MONEY-WISE MAKEOVERS

Copyright © 2010 Filipacchi Publishing,
a division of Hachette Filipacchi Media
U.S., Inc.

First published in 2010 in the United
States of America by Filipacchi Publishing
1633 Broadway
New York, NY 10019

PointClickHome.com is a registered
trademark of Hachette Filipacchi Media
U.S., Inc.

Design: Patricia Fabricant
Editor: Lauren Kuczala
Production: Lynn Scaglione and
Annie Andres

ISBN-13: 978-1-933231-71-6
Library of Congress Control Number:
2009938283

Printed in China

MONEY-WISE MAKEOVERS

Modest Remodels and Affordable Room Redos That Add Value and Improve the Quality of Your Life

JEAN NAYAR

POINTclick**HOME**

Contents

Introduction

LIFE CHANGES, AND SOMETIMES A HOUSE NEEDS to change, too. Maybe you've moved into an existing home designed for another family or another era. Maybe you live in a house that guzzles energy and drains your resources. Or maybe you've simply outgrown the home you have, but don't want to leave it. In any case, there's no reason to let an imperfect home compromise the way you live.

In fact, there's hardly been a better time to upgrade an existing home and improve its value without excessive spending. With the rate of new home construction remaining low, suppliers, contractors and craftspeople are now more available and more amenable to negotiating their rates—even for small projects—than they have been in a long time. And ever-evolving tax incentives and rebates reduce costs and increase payoffs even more.

Whether you want to give a room a lift with low-cost cosmetic changes or give it a whole new life with investment-level structural changes, the money-wise room redos profiled in this book offer insight into a variety of value-conscious ways to enhance your home and improve the way you live for price tags that work for various budgets and goals. Plus, a wealth of eco-friendly ideas, practical energy-saving tips and smart storage solutions will boost your ability to live well—and wisely—in a home that works for today's lifestyles in today's global environment.

JEAN NAYAR

LIVING SPACES

IMPROVING THE QUALITY OF THE LIVING SPACES of your home can be as simple as rearranging furniture and applying a fresh coat of paint, or as demanding as tearing down walls and installing new windows. Whether you opt for basic surface treatments or a substantial rehab will depend upon your budget, of course, as well as your short- and long-term goals. But whatever the case, it helps to begin by studying your room's strengths and weaknesses and looking to the experience of others for ways to play up its attributes and minimize or eliminate its shortcomings.

Your home may be in a wonderful location with spectacular views and yet be completely devoid of character. On the other hand, it may be brimming with character but have oddly configured rooms or spaces that are too small. Or the living areas in your home may be too large, or they simply may not suit your style or your lifestyle.

On the pages that follow, you'll see how various designers and homeowners turned less-than-ideal living rooms, family rooms, dens and home offices into uplifting, functional spaces that accommodate their needs and reflect their tastes. Some projects involved substantial investments aimed at improving the long-term value of the home. Others involved minor upgrades or modest investments in furnishings to make the rooms more livable and enhance the owners' immediate quality of life. All offer solutions to common problems that can be applied to rooms of any style or size in most any location.

Sidelights flanking the front door of this home in a Chicago suburb brighten the front hall. The doorknocker is a replica of a Nantucket basket. Painted wall paneling, which rises to the full height of the door, adds character, while a casual, flat-weave rug injects warmth underfoot. The table—on display as is, water spots and all— holds part of the owner's collection of shell vases and boxes, many of which store tiny items.

Creating Welcoming Entrances

Not every home needs a grand entrance, but a welcoming one is always good. The front door of your home—the primary link between outdoors and in—offers an opportunity to establish an appealing first impression. A good front door should not only harmonize with the exterior character of a home but also reflect something of the spirit of the interior and the personal style of its inhabitants.

Painting a door a cheerful shade of red or an interesting shade of blue is one of the simplest ways to add personality to the face of your home and turn your front door into a focal point. Other low-cost, modest upgrades that will enhance the character of a front door and make it more welcoming include brightening it with lanterns, lending it personality with a creative doorknocker, increasing its stature with a substantial door handle, or making it more inviting with sidelights or a transom. Installing a new door altogether will enrich the character of your home as well as save you money over the long haul by making it more energy-efficient, too. And if you do so before the end of 2010, you may also qualify for a federal tax credit (see sidebar page 18).

Regardless of the style of your front door, it serves as a segue between the exterior and interior, and as such acts as a stylistic transition element into the entrance hall, foyer or landing of your home. Ideally, the character of the front door—or side or back doors or even interior doors leading to and from a garage, for that matter—will complement not only the exterior of your home but also the wall surfaces, furnishings and flooring in the area just beyond it. And the surfaces and furnishings of entrance areas should also be chosen and placed to ease the transition from the outdoors in, or indoors out. You can affordably add style and function to a foyer, entrance hall or mudroom, for example, with simple accents and furnishings, such as pendant light fixtures or chandeliers, peg rails, boot bins, door mats, runners, umbrella stands, storage benches, consoles and hall tables. More ambitious entrance area projects that cost more but can add more value include installing durable stone flooring, adding wall paneling or wainscoting, and building in closets, benches and storage shelves.

Installing new garage doors can also add value by enhancing the character and curb appeal of your home, as well as its energy efficiency. And now that two- and even three-car garages are commonplace, the primary entrance to many American households is through an interior garage door. As such, upgrades to the interior of the garage itself, such as staining or coating concrete floors (see page 135 in chapter 6 for more information) or installing lockers, ceiling racks and other storage elements, can make everyday access to the home more appealing and manageable. You can also cost-effectively enhance the safety of your home at its entry points with technological advancements, such as upgraded garage door openers or integrated security systems, which can cost as little as $100.

BEFORE

above Overgrown shrubs surrounded the old stoop of a ranch house in Portland, Oregon. **below** Architect Yianni Doulis enhanced the facade by installing a new front door and porch deck built of ipe wood, and a pergola of cedar certified by the Forest Stewardship Council. The home's old battleship-gray paint was updated with a lighter, sandy shade. Doulis deftly added architectural oomph to the roofline simply by painting the fascia.

Mudrooms

For most of us, our entryway is just a place we pass through, leaving a trail of shoes and bags behind us. But it's often the first and last thing guests see when they visit, so it sets the tone for the rest of your home. How do you reclaim your mudroom and give it an attractive, welcoming atmosphere?

First step: Create a blank slate. Remove everything and purge—be ruthless and donate things you don't use. Next, corral and conceal what's left over with a storage system and cleaning routine that's right for you. Whether you have an entire room or an entryway wall, here are some ideas to get you started.

- Get your coats in check. Replace flimsy, mismatched hangers with a sturdy wooden set for a uniform look.
- Designate a pretty ceramic dish or a row of hooks near the front door as the parking space for keys.
- Treat your pooch to a cute canine catchall—a container to store leashes, toys and other accoutrements.
- Install slim brackets and a curtain rod on the back of the closet door. Draped scarves look decorative, not messy.
- Prevent mail from piling up. Recycle junk mail right away and cancel unwanted catalogs at *catalogchoice.org*
- Repurpose an old bureau as a place to store winter garb. Use acrylic drawer dividers or cardboard boxes to separate scarves, hats and gloves.

Doors of Distinction
EIGHT PERIOD-APPROPRIATE ARCHITECTURAL DOOR STYLES

DUTCH COLONIAL 1625–1840
Divided so each half can open independently. The top could let in light and air while the bottom stayed closed to keep animals out.

GEORGIAN 1700–1780
Has six or more door panels. The pediment—gabled (shown), segmental, ogee or broken—is a major element of this door. The design often includes pilasters.

FEDERAL 1780–1820 Similar in some ways to the Georgian style. It is also a paneled door, usually with a semicircular fanlight (shown), sidelights and elaborate carving.

GREEK REVIVAL 1825–1860 This style most often had two, four or eight panels with a narrow transom and sidelights. Framed by a cornice, frieze, columns and other decorative elements.

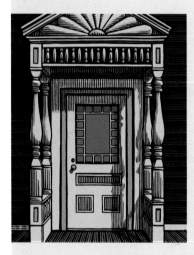

QUEEN ANNE 1880–1910
Paneled wood, typically with a large center glass pane surrounded by smaller ones. Gables are often elaborately decorated. May have turned columns.

TUDOR REVIVAL 1890–1940
Commonly board and batten with round arched tops or Tudor (flattened pointed) arches. Heavy wrought-iron hardware often used.

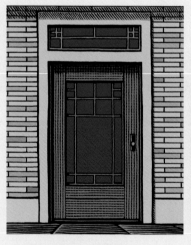

PRAIRIE 1900–1920
Minimally ornamented wood with full panel of decorated lead or stained glass and horizontal rails above and below the panes.

CRAFTSMAN 1905–1930
Flat-panel construction with simple geometric designs and small squares of glass at the top. Sometimes has a small bracketed shelf; often with side panels.

Shopping for Exterior Doors

Just like clothing, the front of a house can make a memorable first impression. Everything from roofing to shutters contributes to a house's vibe, or what real estate brokers call curb appeal. And the front door is often the center of attention. It is, after all, where visitors first make contact with your home.

Your door also provides important architectural clues to what's inside—or at least it should. Whether your house is Federal or Dutch Colonial, the front door is an integral part of the design package.

Doors also have an obvious practical role. A door that can't control temperature extremes isn't much good, no matter how appealing it may be visually. As with many products for the home, exterior doors are given ratings through the federal government's Energy Star program. But keep in mind that ratings are based on climate zone—so a door that is Energy Star–rated for Florida may not be right for your home in Vermont. Check the label to see if the door you're interested in is right for your climate. Here's what you need to know to narrow your options.

WOOD In part due to architectural tradition, wood has long been the material of choice for exterior doors. But wood is also a favored choice because it is available in such a wide range of colors, textures and grain patterns. Since wood is relatively easy to work with, custom wooden doors can be ordered from a local millwork shop as well as from large manufacturers. Size, glass inserts, molding and trim can all be individually specified.

There are drawbacks, though, to wooden doors. Long-term exposure to sunlight, rain and snow exacts its price on wood, particularly those doors with southern and western exposures. Some types of wood, such as mahogany and cedar, are naturally more weather-resistant than others, but all wood is susceptible to warping and decay over time.

As a hedge against the weather, manufacturers such as Kolbe & Kolbe offer wooden doors clad in aluminum with a factory-applied paint finish on the outside and a choice of wood species on the inside. Manufacturers also may combine solid and engineered wood products to reduce the risk of warping. TruStile makes exterior doors entirely from medium-density fiberboard, or MDF. The keys to long life for a natural or engineered-wood door? Maintain the finish and protect it from extreme sun and rain.

FIBERGLASS Thanks to realistic grain rendering and colors that mimic natural wood tones, fiberglass doors look a lot like wood.

But fiberglass is not nearly as likely to be damaged by weather exposure as wood. Fiberglass doors typically cost less than top-of-the-line wood styles, and a foam core makes them much better insulators than plain wood. This tough and resilient material also holds up well to bumps and dings, making it a low-maintenance option with plenty of eye appeal.

However, because of the way fiberglass doors are manufactured, they can't be customized as easily as wood. Yet there are scores of styles to choose from and plenty of options for sidelights, glass inserts and transoms.

STEEL Steel doors have two advantages: They're usually the least expensive and, like fiberglass doors, they have a foam core that makes them much better thermal insulators than wood.

The main complaint about steel doors is that the outer faces are relatively thin, meaning dings and dents are always a risk. Minor flaws can be repaired, but the material is inherently less resilient than the other options. Rust is a risk if the finish is damaged and not repaired or if the door isn't protected from rain and snow by a porch or portico.

All but the most basic doors come with a choice of windows, sidelights and transoms, not to mention hardware. Once you know the material that best suits your climate and budget, it'll be easier to find a door that will keep out the elements—and suit your house's style.

Enhancing Living and Family Rooms, Dens and Home Offices

Large or small, modern or traditional, formal or casual, living rooms and family rooms are the primary gathering spaces of a home. The best living spaces are situated, configured, furnished and finished out to support their owners' lifestyles, personal tastes and practical needs. The same holds true for dens and home offices, a home's more utilitarian, and usually more personal, living spaces. Shaping these spaces to perform at their optimum may involve enlisting the help of an architect, designer or contractor. In other cases, a little DIY effort is all that's required. On the pages that follow, a variety of value-conscious strategies employed by a wide range of homeowners and designers offer inspiration and practical wisdom that can be applied to your own living spaces.

Opening Up and Maximizing Views

Unlike a decorator who designs other people's houses, Jeff Lewis, a Los Angeles real estate developer, serial renovator and host of the popular Bravo TV show *Flipping Out,* usually lives in a house as he redoes it, and then sells it. Over the course of 10 years, he's lived in 30 different houses, so he's gained ample insight into what makes a house work—or not. And his approach to designing rooms is about making changes that will increase a home's resale value as much as they will its comfort.

When his current 3,000-square-foot house in Los Feliz, California, a trendy, woodsy neighborhood near Griffith Park and downtown Los Angeles, came on the market in 2006, he kept his eye on it for nearly a year, patiently waiting out price reductions and rejected offers until he finally nabbed it after the price dropped by almost 30 percent. Then he and his business partner, Ryan Brown, completely revamped it.

According to Lewis, who believes in making houses feel airy and filled with natural light, the house, which was originally built in 1963, failed to make the most of the attributes of its site. "I felt this house was all about the view," says Lewis, "so we took down a wall that was blocking the living room views from the landing, and also opened up the kitchen to the living room." The two men also replaced the house's old windows with seven sets of sliding pocket doors, opening up the house so "it feels like a grownup treehouse," says Lewis. Creating a more open space plan brightened the living space considerably, but Lewis made other modest alterations to enhance the light, airy qualities he desired. "If this house has one limitation, it's that the ceilings are standard height," he says, "but we made them feel taller by painting all the dark-wood ceiling beams white, and enlarging and raising door openings."

Clean-lined, minimalist furnishings and accents also help achieve a sense of spaciousness. "The less furniture, the better," he says. "You don't have to put something in every corner or on every blank wall. If I have an inkling that it looks cluttered, I take stuff away."

Energy Smarts

Ever forget to turn off the air-conditioning (or turn down the heat) when you leave in the morning? Programmable thermostats solve this problem by letting you set the temperature for different times of day. Depending on the model, you can program the same settings for every day or employ different settings for weekdays and weekends.

Between 40 and 70 percent of people who own programmable thermostats don't use them properly. The best way to do it is to figure out your schedule—when you're home, at work and sleeping—then set your thermostat and leave it alone. Energy experts recommend these settings:

	WINTER	SUMMER
Rise and shine	70°F	78°F
Off to work	62°F	85°F
Home for dinner	70°F	78°F
Sweet dreams	62°F	82°F

Owner Jeff Lewis opened up his living room by taking out a wall and closet that blocked views upon entry from the landing. The living/dining room and public rooms on the second floor open onto expansive views that give a sense of being "on top of the world." Modern furniture in solid hues grounds the room yet keeps it feeling airy. The wood-veneer fireplace wall and ottomans add drama to the neutral scheme, as does the painting by Matthew Ehrmann.

Revamping Within an Existing Footprint
TAKING A DIY APPROACH

In search of some respite from full-time city life in downtown Manhattan, Mel and Jean Furukawa bought a tiny shingled weekend house in the hamlet of Noyack in the Hamptons, an area known more for its manicured hedges and costly houses than its Lilliputian fishing shacks. Nestled off a quiet country lane near Noyack Bay, the Furukawas' three-bedroom house, built in 1959, was in total disrepair when the couple found it—the previous owners had abandoned a series of improvements midway through. But Mel and Jean saw its potential, and working within the existing 1,000-square-foot layout and on a bare-bones budget, they started by making a few structural upgrades, doing much of the work themselves.

   To create a greater sense of expansiveness in the compact primary ground-floor living room, they opened it up by tearing out the wall that separated it from the kitchen, and replaced its bay window with French doors that open to the outdoors. To make the room warmer and more inviting, they covered its worn linoleum floors, as well as those throughout the house, upstairs and down, with 12-inch-wide pine planks. Over the course of two decades, they shaped the interiors with a few low-cost new pieces mixed with a

carefully edited collection of curios and castoff furnishings they gathered from flea markets and sidewalks, and defined a humbly artful space that is easy to maintain and very personal, too. Much of the furniture is also lightweight, portable or foldable, which keeps the diminutive rooms from feeling overcrowded.

WORKING WITH AN ARCHITECT

above The wicker sofa was a flea-market find; the upholstered pieces are from West Elm. "The new furniture adds freshness," says owner Jean Furukawa. The standing lamp is from the town dump; the sculptural wicker ottoman was a $5 yard-sale find. above right A desk separates the kitchen and living areas. The couple gave the $9 Ikea wicker chair a style upgrade with pale celery paint. A gauzy curtain lets the living room double as a sleeping area for houseguests.

Frank and Maria Chiodi, new homeowners in East Hampton, New York, worked with LEED-accredited architect Joseph Eisner to overhaul their 1980s house, "which was in dire need of updating," the architect says. Tackling it in stages and with green design in mind, Eisner introduced upgrades that transformed the lackluster house into an inviting retreat from work life in Manhattan. "Rather than raze the structure, which is common in the Hamptons, adapting the house within its original footprint was in itself a conservation strategy," he says. "And for the new construction we employed sustainable materials throughout the house."

The overhaul of the first-floor living area involved incorporating a pass-through room divider to separate the living room from a new U-shaped kitchen plan that opens onto it. Clad in Lyptus, a hybrid hardwood grown in managed-growth forests, the divider has a credenza-like feeling and creates a sense of visual continuity with new cabinets and other elements in different areas of the house also made of the same material. A second-floor balcony that overlooks the room gained architectural heft with a similar wood treatment supported by blackened metal hardware.

Efficient new windows and sliding doors make it easier to appreciate and access exterior improvements, including a new deck and enhanced pool area. "I wanted to create an indoor/outdoor garden sensibility, visually connecting the two areas," Eisner says. Eco-friendly finishes—low-VOC paints and stains—were also used in the living area and throughout the house. "There's a significantly better flow for entertaining with the kitchen now open to the living room and deck, just outside," Frank says. Merging indoor and outdoor living, this updated house now weds modern architectural forms with tactile materials.

above Before the renovation, the dining room was open to the living room and outdated kitchen. The staircase had been enclosed, blocking light. A boxy wallboard balcony enclosure and bland walls in the living room lacked visual interest.

above New windows frame the view of garden architecture, decks and twin cabanas, at home in the landscape. left Built-in shelving and storage units in the living room are fabricated from Lyptus, a hybrid hardwood. Architect Joseph Eisner linked the second floor to the space by wrapping the balcony with it as well.

Low-VOC paints and floor finishes gave this home office, which had been a spare bedroom, an eco-friendly update. Compact fluorescent bulbs provide energy-efficient illumination.

Eco-Friendly, Moneywise Tips

Cutting back on energy consumption is a big priority for most Americans. The good news is that many home energy-saving strategies are really easy to pull off. What's more, the ones that are pricey and/or labor-intensive are typically the ones that pay off the most in the long haul—and make you feel like a responsible citizen.

- **MAKE AN UPGRADE AND SAVE TWICE.** If you've been dragging your heels on a green remodeling project, tax credits of up to $500 for energy-efficient home improvements may inspire you to follow through on it. If you install new energy-efficient windows, doors, roofs, insulation, heating and cooling systems, and/or water heaters before the end of 2010, you may qualify for a federal tax credit. For a full list of qualifying improvements and more information, visit *energystar.gov* and click on "Tax Credits for Energy Efficiency."

- **TAKE THE ALTERNATIVE ROUTE.** If customers so request, many electric utilities will deliver power from eco-friendly energy sources, including wind, solar and others, at a modest premium. Check out *eere.energy.gov/greenpower* for options in each state.

- **REPLACE WINDOWS.** If your windows put just one sheet of glass between you and the outside, you should replace them. Double-glazed windows typically feature a low-emissivity (low-E) coating, and the gap between the sheets of glass is filled with an insulating gas (usually argon). These windows mitigate heat loss in cold weather, and depending on the region of the country, they usher in or ward off the sun's heat. If you have a double-glazed window and you see condensation between the glass, it means the seal has broken and you should replace that window.

- **CHECK THE SEAL.** Exterior air leaks—around windows, doors, ventilation fans, etc.—can force heating and air conditioning systems to work harder, using more energy. A home-energy audit performed by a professional technician can spot these air leaks, along with areas of inadequate insulation. While tending to the exterior, homeowners should also inspect heating and cooling ducts. Leaks within these systems are energy wasters, too. Start with your local power utility to find an energy audit technician.

- **DETOX YOUR WALLS.** Visit *greenwisepaint.com* before you start your project for a listing of brands that offer low-VOC paints that meet stringent criteria for performance as well as environmental standards. They won't release harmful gases into your home—or the atmosphere. Try Elements Zero VOC paints, $35 to $40 per gallon; 800-225-1141, *californiapaints.com* for stores.

- **ADD CURTAINS.** You can enhance the insulation value of any window with the right window treatment. Some draperies are designed as thermal barriers, but you can also add an insulating layer, such as a napped lining, to standard curtains. The idea is to keep the heavier cool air near the window from entering the heated room. Layering curtains over shades provides additional insulation, too.

- **CHOOSE THE RIGHT LIGHT.** Compact fluorescent lamps (CFLs) have been much publicized in the past year, and for good reason. They really do save lots of energy over ordinary incandescent bulbs. Earlier types of CFLs gave off a harsher light, but the newest versions are more like incandescents. The government says one household CFL, over its lifetime, can save $30 in electricity over a comparable incandescent bulb.

- **REPLACE OLD FILTERS.** This is an easy one. Filters for heating and air-conditioning systems are inexpensive and easy to replace. The cleaner the filter, the more efficiently the system runs.

Adding On and Enhancing Existing Spaces

With three young children, Andrea and Chris Roberson wanted a home with a practical floor plan and durable finishes and furnishings that would stand up to daily wear and tear, yet still look neat and stylish. When they found a small 1940s house on a vast wooded lot in a good neighborhood in suburban Washington, DC, they snapped it up with intentions of renovating the quirky property to suit their growing family. After moving in, they enlisted their new neighbor, architect Charles Moore, to help them transform the compact house into the 3,000-square-foot, four-bedroom, Arts and Crafts–inspired cottage they desired.

"The original house had major aesthetic and functional issues, and no basement, so storage was also a priority," says Moore. "We needed to increase the size and improve the look without tearing it down." Moore's new plan expanded the home's second story, and added a new kitchen, family room and dining room wing, accessed by a long, gallery-style hallway, which provides a direct route from the rear mudroom to the main staircase near the front door. "It's the most important thing we added," says Andrea of the passageway. "We knew we'd have lots of little ones underfoot, and we didn't want them cutting through rooms and running past furniture." All of that traffic required a tough material underfoot, too, so Andrea chose a limestone tile that has the look of old Italian cobblestones and enriches the character of the house. "If that had been a wooden floor, it would be partially destroyed by now," adds Moore.

The home's original living room had good bones, nice light, and was spacious, so they kept it intact, only adding architectural character with a coffered ceiling treatment. Divided into two zones—a small reading nook and a main seating area around the fireplace—it's a great place to sit and talk or play a game. To brighten the space, the owners added a mix of contemporary and traditional furnishings, classic finishes and fresh color. Shutters were added to the windows as a low-maintenance way to control light and privacy.

This formal living room is outfitted with matching dark green velvet sofas, a bench covered in a cotton/linen-blend fabric, and a large, synthetic area rug that's easy to keep clean. "We chose to use mostly neutrals, and play with color in the pillow fabric," says owner Andrea Roberson. Architectural coffers were added to lend character to the space.

Redefining the Character of a 1970s A-Frame

ON THE EAST COAST WITH CLASSIC SHINGLE STYLE

A 1970s A-frame house doesn't exactly conjure a vision of traditional warmth and coziness. But in the hands of homeowner Elaine Dia and her husband, Scott, a neglected 40-year-old structure in the Hamptons morphed into a classic yet fresh Shingle-style retreat, with colors inspired by the nearby seacoast.

"It looked more like a ski chalet than a beach cottage," says Elaine. "I wanted the house to sit on the land properly." So five years ago, Elaine took on the redo, borrowing ideas and inspiration from nearby cottages. To make the house's exterior look less A-shaped—both ends of the roof had extended all the way to the ground—Elaine had the sides cut back and the facade shingled with Alaskan cedar shakes. Inside, she had the home gutted and the living room lengthened by 10 feet, with a full-width entry deck added outside. The new plan opened living areas to one another, including a compact kitchen, which opens into the living and dining areas and has views of the deck and trees.

Elaine's design goal was to keep rooms clean and organic, with ocean-inspired colors reminiscent of beach glass. She grounded her design and color scheme with cherry wood flooring, windows covered with simple whitewashed matchstick blinds, and walls painted in the palest shades of grays, greens and blues. To keep housekeeping chores simple, couches and chairs are covered with washable slipcovers, and floors with sturdy jute rugs. Even though she worked within a budget, Elaine wanted furniture with a history, which in her case often meant things that nature has left behind. A living room side table, for instance, is topped with shells the couple collected on the beach. Pieces of driftwood show up unexpectedly in sculpture or attached to a light fixture. For objects that have a human history, pedigree didn't matter: Scott and Elaine rehabbed a chest, now in their living room, that they rescued from a New York City sidewalk.

The couple also got lucky with some of the previous owners' leftover items. "The classic Wegner chair in the living room was just left here," says Elaine. And the coffee table was made from a giant slab of slate that had been outdoors, sitting on a rusty base in lieu of a picnic table. Elaine planned to keep it that way, but during the remodel, the piece was dropped and damaged. "The accident left the slate with a beautifully broken edge," she says. "It was a natural for becoming the top for our new coffee table."

Space-Saving Dos & Don'ts

- **DO PLAN AHEAD.** Grab a pad of paper and walk around the house with a fresh eye, noting where you might be able to add storage you hadn't thought of before.
- **DON'T HOLD ON TO THE PAST.** If you haven't used it, needed it, or admired it in the last 12 months, say adios!
- **DO TAKE ADVANTAGE OF LEDGES AND ALCOVES.** Often wasted, these spaces are perfect for adding cubbies or shelving. You can also build niches in the area between wall studs.
- **DON'T BE AFRAID OF HEIGHTS.** Take advantage of vertical space by installing an extra-tall freestanding bookcase or cabinet (be sure to follow instructions and anchor it properly to the wall).
- **DO USE PRACTICAL PIECES.** Nesting tables and benches are great options for small living rooms. Tuck them under each other to give yourself some breathing room, then separate them when needed.
- **DON'T LIMIT YOUR THINKING.** Let your home office double as a guest bedroom. A trundle bed is a great way to add a sleeping spot for visitors. Comfy chairs that flip out into twin beds, slender futons and even a new generation of Murphy beds are all ways to conserve space in a home office/guest room.
- **DO DOUBLE DUTY.** The hidden compartment in a storage ottoman can hide a blanket and pillow, or hold games, videos or seasonal gear. Bonus ideas: Place three together under a window for an instant bench, or put two in front of a sofa for a snazzy upholstered coffee table.
- **DON'T LOSE SIGHT OF THE WINDOWS.** Make the most of a dormer by adding a window seat with drawers. Or build a window seat in front of a larger window and incorporate storage bins or drawers underneath.
- **DO WATCH YOUR STEPS.** The underside of a staircase is often overlooked, but it's perfect for shelves or a half-closet. You may even be able to create a powder room.

opposite Comfortable living-room furniture is slipcovered in washable fabrics. The Danish-modern rope chair was left behind by former owners. Jute rugs, matchstick blinds and a shell-topped table give the room the casual, beachy feel homeowners Elaine and Scott Dia wanted in what had been an A-frame house. The couple cut off the sides of the roof and turned the home into a Shingle-style structure, more reflective of those in its environs.

Furnishing a Large Family Room for under $6,000

To make this ultra-large family room feel cozier, all of the furnishings were pulled away from the walls and floated in the middle of the room around its centerpiece—the massive stone fireplace. The large-scale pieces ideally complement the scale of the setting, and the affordable faux leather chairs and faux suede sofa are super-easy to care for, too.

In this family room, the club chairs are actually recliners that combine traditional style and comfort. The leather sofa is topped with microfiber-upholstered cushions and pillows that are easy-care while offering the look of suede. The center ottoman functions as a coffee table or additional cozy seating in front of the fireplace. The bright graphic pattern of the rug offers a contrast to the strong profiles of the furnishings. A lamp and pillows pick up the red of the rug for added visual punch. A gutsy, wide-framed mirror over the fireplace reflects light and draws the eye toward the rock surround.

The Tab

Sectional sofa	$1,900
Two armchair recliners	$1,400
Rug	$1,210
Ottoman	$600
Mirror	$240
Lamp	$135
Two throw blankets	$129
Vases on mantel	$117
Side table	$115
Two red throw pillows	$58
Two fireplace baskets	$34
Four Roman shades	$32
TOTAL:	**$5,970**

ON THE WEST COAST WITH CONTEMPORARY STYLE

After collaborating on rehabbing and selling other houses on the Oregon coast, graphic and interior designer Pamela Hill and her colleague, friend and neighbor, architect Lois Mackenzie, decided to buy one together and revamp it into a weekend house their two families could share. They found a well-situated but dated two-bedroom A-frame on Arch Cape, a tiny coastal town a little over an hour west of their homes in Portland. "This house is on a double lot, with 100 feet of beachfront, but it still feels private," says Pamela.

The previous owner built it himself in 1972, and it was all wood, inside and out. "It was really dark and dated, and the windows cut off the view," she says. To brighten and bring it up to date and maximize the panoramic ocean view, Pamela and Lois redid the front of the house, replacing and enlarging the windows and raising them a foot higher. They also painted all the woodwork white, including the ceiling, which lightened and refreshed the space dramatically.

A massive stone fireplace also dominated and darkened the room. Lois and Pamela ripped it out, replacing the stone with matte white '50s-inspired oval ceramic tile. "It's utilitarian but beautiful," says Pamela, "which is the whole point of our designs." They also tucked in a reading nook beside the fireplace, with an upholstered bench and storage underneath. "It's all about capturing space wherever you can in a small house like this," says Lois.

The two friends kept the furnishings clean and simple. "We created a color story," says Pamela. "It has a way of pulling a house together." Here, it's white, warm gray, red and chocolate. The pops of red—in a classic Eero Saarinen Womb chair in the living room and zippy pillows throughout—give a jolt to the otherwise quiet white-and-gray scheme. Pamela deftly balanced inexpensive basics from Ikea with a few signature pieces, like the Saarinen chair. "We think of our style as timeless, modern, organic design," says Pamela. "We put our money into the things that will last the longest—stone, tile, fixtures." They also focused their budget on the living room, and kept the bedrooms relatively small and spare.

below left Vintage chairs, spray-painted white, are draped with fur and pulled up to a tree-stump table created by Lois's husband, Kevin, an arborist, for a front-row seat on the ocean. below right Low-slung, clean-lined furnishings are sparked by Eero Saarinen's red Womb chair and the lush texture of a flokati rug. The coffee table was a vintage find. Heath Ceramic tiles, originally designed in the 1950s, clad the fireplace wall, atop a concrete surround.

Freshening Up an Old Room

With its tall, leaded windows and wood paneling, the architectural elements of this room in an old house in Mill Neck, New York, threatened to overpower the modern furnishings in the main seating area. To showcase these features more subtly, designer Eileen Kathryn Boyd painted the walls and moldings soft gray and added visual interest to the ceiling with a gray patterned wallcovering. To enable the furnishings to stand out, Boyd employed bold color and graphic pattern inspired by the sunny floral pattern on a shirt she wore while studying in Paris several years ago.

Boyd knew the color would work well in this expansive sitting room, but was also aware of the challenge it represented. "I wanted the yellow to play an important part," says Boyd, "but in a way that was fresh, stylish and modern for today." The subdued French gray surfaces and accents in robin's-egg blue proved the perfect counterpoints. Laced with artfully employed trims and thoughtful decorative touches, the room brims with contemporary elegance.

The key to achieving color balance, says Boyd, is to use your base color for two-thirds of the room and your brightest color for the other third. Choose a main accent color, then use its opposite (complementary) color on the color wheel for harmonious effect. Here, the blue lamp and throw pillow offset the hand-painted yellow mirror frame perfectly. White accents throughout give the eye places to rest.

above left Yellow binding tape was added around the border of the sisal rug to unify the color throughout the room. "Rug companies already have these colorful binding tapes available," says Boyd, "though few people ever take advantage of it. All you have to do is ask."
above center To highlight the century-old room's geometrical architecture, Boyd created a square painting featuring the same flower that inspired the room's color palette.
above right With its tall leaded windows and wood paneling, the room's architectural elements threatened to overpower the modern furnishings. To showcase these features more subtly, the designer painted walls a soft gray and applied a patterned wallpaper to the ceiling. Grosgrain ribbon highlights the curtains.

Creating Character in Featureless Rooms
WITH FURNITURE AND ACCENTS

Designer Kate Singer's 1950s home in Huntington, New York, overlooks an all-American view across Long Island Sound. Inside, though, its rooms reveal Kate's love of things French combined with the natural colors of the countryside. "I've always lived near the water, so I gravitate toward the colors of the shore," says Kate, owner of Kate Singer Home. Her fondness for French style is a taste she acquired on her travels in Europe. And the home she's created for her husband, Scott, and two daughters is a serene blend of the two, with a changing assortment of collectibles displayed throughout.

Over the years, Kate has picked up collections of mercury glass, silver, alabaster, starburst convex mirrors and brown transferware. The furnishings she's acquired reflect her preference for simple lines and traditional design and include a few bargain finds that have been lovingly refurbished to fit the decor.

The living room, with its shades of sand, brown and blue, sets the tone for the home's decor—uncluttered and comfortable. A rich, subtle area rug grounds the room's seating arrangements, including a custom-designed corner where she showcases some of her French artwork and collectibles. "It was an awkward corner," says Kate, "where no one ever sat." To remedy the problem, Kate transformed the corner into an inviting niche with a custom-built banquette, like one in a French salon. In the cooler months, she switches out the coffee table for a small round table.

above left To increase the character quotient in the living room of her 1950s home, designer Kate Singer added muntins to the plain casement windows and installed crown moldings around the ceiling. To enhance the sense of height in the low-ceilinged room, she installed the curtain rod just below the crown molding, which lifts the eye up and makes the room feel grander.
above right Vintage French portraits and landscapes mingle with a collection of cameos above the living room's custom banquette. Wall sconces brighten the area for reading or games.
below An antique desk provides a compact work area that complements the elegant style of the living room and folds up neatly when not in use.

Easy Ways to Add Character

With basic white walls and run-of-the-mill fixtures, most newly constructed homes could use a big dose of personality. What are the keys to imprinting your personal style to create instant character? Here, three clever interiors experts provide some design inspiration.

- **CONSIDER THE DETAILS.** A few well-placed architectural details can turn a bland room into a grand room. Add dimension to a ceiling with coffers or beams. "This is a great way to define different sections of large spaces, such as a kitchen, dining or great room," says Richmond, Virginia–based interior designer Marcie Blough.

- **LOOK FOR WINDOWS OF OPPORTUNITY.** Framing a window with the right treatment makes a marked improvement in the finish level of a new room. "It's easy to add drama, color, and detail with drapery hardware and great fabrics," says interior designer Kathryn Chaplow of Grand Rapids, Michigan. Mount treatments several inches above the window casings for added height.

- **COLOR YOUR WORLD.** Painting is the fastest way to enhance the look of a room, and a little color in an unexpected place can make a big impact. "I love interior doors painted a contrasting color," says Chaplow. "Black doors in a house with all white trim are so chic, and touches like that provide an instant sense of customization and history."

- **MIND THE SCALE.** Many new homes have high-volume ceilings, so it's important to maintain balance in the space below.

"Nothing makes a big room look disproportionately large like tiny furnishings and accessories," says Chaplow. For large walls with little detail or trim work, try a grouping of nicely framed art or a grand framed mirror. "Remember to keep accessories focused, and in proportion to the size of the area," the designer notes. "A lot of small things can become clutter rather than points of interest."

- **LIGHTEN UP.** The right (or wrong) lighting can instantly change the mood of a space. "Ideally, a room should have three types of lighting," says Blough. "Ambient (overhead), task (focused on an area for a specific activity) and accent lighting (such as a sconce) add interest." Pendants over a kitchen island, sconces in a bathroom, a striking foyer fixture or small LEDs in built-in bookshelves can add instant light and life. Or try directional lighting in a hallway for a cool, gallery effect. Neutrals paired with jolts of color and pattern create a serene but interesting space.

- **MIX IT UP.** A blend of eclectic furnishings and accessories can give a new home a cozy, lived-in look. When designing the interiors for a custom home, Skye Kirby of Lillian August in Norwalk, Connecticut, spiced up the palette of creams, grays and golds with pops of black and small touches of animal print. "A little bit of zebra goes a long way," Kirby says. She also maintained a proper balance of new and old-looking pieces by introducing a rustic cabinet with vintage glass doors to the tailored family room.

WITH AFFORDABLE FINISHES AND ARCHITECTURAL DETAILS

Renowned for his deft use of texture, color and scale, interior designer T. Keller Donovan recently applied his signature tailored style to a Pennsylvania couple's second home in Lake Worth, Florida. The 2,300-square-foot, three-bedroom house had the advantages of a nicely flowing floor plan and 11-foot ceilings. But, being a builder's spec house, it had a "cookie-cutter feeling," Donovan says. So the designer introduced some simple interior upgrades to inject the rooms with sophisticated yet spirited flavor. "The rooms were generously sized, but needed architectural details, like moldings and shutters, to create spaces with an inviting, human scale," he says.

"We wanted a house that was warm and welcoming, without being too fussy," says the owner. Taking a cue from the Florida locale, Donovan worked with a sand-and-sea palette of textured neutral surfaces and finishes infused with graphic punches of blue and white. Cool and classic, the limited palette ties the rooms together with a calming sense of continuity. He started by installing ceramic tile floors in a sandy hue to ground the spaces with a visual flow throughout. To add architectural interest, Donovan added white plantation-style shutters to the windows in most rooms. "It's an easy-to-maintain, crisp look that is streamlined and evokes the Florida locale," Donovan says. The filtered sunlight also helps regulate the temperature of each room. New ceiling fans enhance the tropical mood, while new white crown moldings accent creamy painted walls for a finished look. And crisp, plush furnishings and boldly patterned accents add a layer of fresh,

classic style. "Keeping fabrics to one or two choices per room creates a modern, tailored feeling," Donovan says.

Wallpaper was another tool the designer employed to enrich the spaces with texture, pattern and personality. In the den, for example, which doubles as a home office, brown wallpaper with a subtle texture makes the space feel like a cozy retreat. White molding, set two feet below the ceiling, visually brings down the scale of the room. Donovan also took out the existing closet to create a niche where the desk now sits. Framed prints of palm trees wrap around the room at eye level to contrast with the dark walls. It's a different look from the creamy-walled backdrops elsewhere in the house, meant to convey a private inner sanctum.

above left Wallcovering warms the den. White molding visually lowers the ceiling. left White plantation shutters, crown molding, a ceiling fan and a large-scale print on the cushions add character in the family room. New shutters emphasize the transom windows above and enhance climate control. Before they were updated, the rooms had a cookie-cutter quality.

Brightening and Adding Value to Dated Spaces Cost-Effectively

After interior designer Pamela Hill and architect Lois Mackenzie purchased a 1940s two-bedroom "beach shack" to fix up and resell, they started by shoring up the house's systems and upgraded its exterior, then they turned their attention to brightening the interior living spaces within a reasonable budget. Their goal was to create a "turnkey" house, fully equipped down to the dishes and shower curtains, and furnished in a fresh, clean style—so a new owner could just move in.

How to spiffily furnish a 1,750-square-foot house on a very tight budget? Inspired by the rocks and light of the romantic coastline, they started by choosing a contemporary palette of gray, white and citrus colors to make the formerly dark-painted rooms feel airy and unified. "We combined luxury items like boutique rugs with thrift-shop and department-store finds," says Pamela. Cost-conscious upgrades included refreshing the walls and brick fireplace surround with a few coats of white paint and adding a reupholstered second-hand sofa. The new red oak floors are second-grade, yet beautiful. Just 16 days after Pamela and Lois put up the For Sale sign back in 2007, a couple peered through the windows and promptly bought the place.

above The living room is narrow, but the Oregon coast is wide, especially when taken in from the reupholstered secondhand sofa and cozy chaises at the window. Architect Lois Mackenzie completely refurbished this "beach shack" with her designer friend, Pamela Hill, for instant, turnkey living. **below** The original living room was dark and cluttered. The view from a bluff on the windy, sea-gouged Oregon coast is spectacular. But the house situated there was another matter.

BEFORE

Working with Paint

CHOOSING A COLOR Color can have an impact on your mood, so choose carefully. Many people prefer the calming effect of cool colors (greens and blues) in bedrooms and private spaces, and energizing warm colors (reds and yellows) in public areas such as living rooms and kitchens. Darker shades usually impart a cozy feeling, while pastels can make a small space feel open and airy. Explore your personal preferences by looking at magazines and model homes for ideas. Many paint manufacturers' websites also offer tools to help you visualize colors in various rooms. One place to start is to select a background color from a fabric or accessory in the room you want to paint; some stores can computer-match colors for an exact match.

Keep in mind that colors on paint chips appear lighter than they will on your walls. It may be wise to invest in a sample before you paint an entire room. Test-paint a small area of the wall or, better yet, paint a piece of plywood that you can move around the space. Observe how the color looks against furniture at various times of the day and in artificial light.

DETERMINING HOW MUCH TO BUY You'll need approximately one gallon of paint to cover 350 square feet of wall surface. You can calculate the amount by multiplying wall height by width, taking open spaces like windows and doorways into consideration.

Along with the room's size, the color you're painting over will determine how much to buy. Painting over a similar shade might take just one coat, while painting light over dark or dark over light may require two or three. Prepare dark walls with a tinted primer that almost matches your paint color for the best coverage.

PREPPING THE ROOM Thinking of skipping the grunt work? Don't. Prepping is key to professional-looking results.

Remove window treatments, pictures and portable furnishings from the room, and move large items away from walls. If you're painting ceilings, take down light fixtures or cover them with plastic, loosening or taking off cover plates to paint beneath them. Switchplates and outlet covers should also be removed (tape screws to plates to keep them organized); if you're painting windows and doors, mask or remove as much hardware as possible. Cover any furniture left in the room with plastic sheets, and spread nonslip canvas drop cloths on the floors. (Use painter's tape to hold it down.)

Preparing walls can be a dusty chore, so ventilate the room with a fan or open windows and wear a mask. Begin by removing nails and screws, then wash walls with a mild solution of household detergent (mildewed areas should first be cleaned with a mild bleach solution). Sponge walls off with clean water. When walls are dry, fill holes and small cracks with spackling compound, smoothing the patches with fine-grit sandpaper when dry. Also sand trim that will be painted to remove surface gloss and flaked paint.

Mask around trim with blue painter's tape to ensure straight lines. To make tape easier to remove, press it down along the paint-side edge, leaving the other edge slightly up.

New walls that have never been painted should be brushed to remove dust, then primed. On walls heavily stained by old leaks, use a stain-blocking primer to prevent discolorations from showing through new paint. (Be sure the leaks have been repaired.)

START PAINTING! If you're painting everything, the sequence is ceiling, walls, then trim. You'll need separate rollers for the ceiling and walls (choose long-napped rollers for heavily textured walls or popcorn ceilings), an extension handle for reaching ceilings, and a chisel-edge brush for painting in corners and along edges. Check with the pro at your home-improvement store for specific items for your project. If you're working on a ladder, choose metal paint trays that can hook on without buckling; covering trays with plastic liners will make cleanup easier.

Fill the paint tray to about a third of its depth. Be careful not to overload rollers and brushes. Rollers should be dipped then rolled along the tray's slanted surface to distribute the paint evenly. Dip

about one third the length of the brushes' bristles into the paint, removing excess paint by tapping the ferrule (the metal ring around bristles) against the can's rim.

If being in a freshly painted room gives you a sore throat, itchy eyes or a headache, you may be reacting to the volatile organic compounds (VOCs) in commercial paints. VOCs are solvents added to paint to give it its consistency. As the paint dries, the VOCs release gases. Exposure to these gases can be especially difficult for environmentally sensitive people or asthma sufferers; long-term exposure can cause health problems.

Painting 101

STEP 1 On ceilings, use a brush to paint around edges, extending the paint several inches onto the ceiling. Then switch to a roller and, beginning in a corner, work in 9- to 12-square-foot sections. Roll a large W shape on the section, then go back and fill it in. As you paint, maintain even pressure without lifting

the roller from the surface. When ceiling paint is dry, mask off perimeter with butcher paper and painter's tape and paint the edges of the walls with a brush.

STEP 2 Using a brush, paint along ceiling lines, in corners and around trim. With a roller, begin in a corner and work from the top down, using the same W technique as for the ceiling. If you're painting trim, wait until wall paint dries and mask off walls next to trimmed elements with painter's tape and butcher paper.

STEP 3 To paint trim, brush in the same direction as the grain of the wood. Doors without panels can be painted with a roller to save time. As you work, check surfaces for drips, smoothing them out as you go. (If you're seeing too many drips, you're overloading the roller or brush with too much paint.)

Conscientious Cleanup

- Wash brushes and rollers in warm, soapy water, then rinse and shake off the excess water.
- To dry, stand the rollers on end and hang the brush by its handle.
- Brushes, with bristles carefully smoothed, can be stored in their original jackets, and rollers in perforated plastic bags.
- Contact your local city or county offices to find out about disposing of paint cans, or visit *epa.gov* for more information.

Earth-Friendly Paint

Many paint manufacturers offer low- or no-VOC alternatives, including Behr's low-VOC paint, Benjamin Moore's Eco Spec, Glidden's Evermore and Sherwin-Williams' GreenSure paints. A Green Seal label indicates that the paint contains a VOC level well below the Environmental Protection Agency's standard. Visit paint manufacturers' sites for product particulars, and check these sites for more information:

> *epa.gov*
> *greenseal.org*
> *eartheasy.com*
> *consumersearch.com*
> *cpsc.gov*

left If you're hesitant to commit to a bold color on all four walls of a room, consider using it on just one wall to create a focal point or accent wall. **opposite** The original living room was so dark that lamps were needed in the middle of the day. The pine wall paneling was kept for added dimension, but was painted white to refresh the space. The mid-century glass coffee table was found at Goodwill and paired with more traditional plaid patterns.

Blurring Boundaries Between Indoors and Out

IN A COTTAGE STYLE

Designer Amanda Sandberg and her husband, Blake, have made it their business to remake houses to feel like getaways all year round. Amanda and Blake are serial renovators: They buy ugly-duckling houses (usually '60s ranches), and while living in the house with their own family, renovate and decorate to create an irresistible idyll. Then they sell the home—furnishings, artwork and all—so the new owners can enjoy the total experience.

In this house, which they renovated over a period of several years and recently sold to a young family, that meant ripping out the outdated kitchen and opening it up to the family and dining rooms, then opening up the whole house to the outdoors, which itself got a major makeover. Amanda employs a simple, consistent color palette to make a house feel open and calming. All the hard surfaces—counters, floors, fixtures—which are typically the hardest to change, are kept neutral, so they work with any scheme. Large upholstered pieces are slipcovered, usually in white. Amanda then chooses a single accent color—in this case, lime green—that she weaves through the main rooms in easily changeable accents: pillows, dishes, throws. "That way if you get tired of the color, it's easy and inexpensive to change," she explains.

The designer also brightened the living room of this California cottage and linked it to the outdoor living space she developed for the home by painting the wall paneling white. Sandberg used jolts of lime green to visually connect a home office area near the kitchen to the living room. Cabinetlike drawers topped with a mahogany desktop lend substance to the space, while relaxed storage baskets and a grid of starfish prints on the wall keep the feeling relaxed.

Relaxed furnishings, sliding doors and slipcovers on furniture reinforce the indoor/outdoor lifestyle preferred by the owner of this Southern California home designed by Amanda Sandberg and her husband, Blake. Keeping accents to a single hue unifies the decor. The accents can also be switched out easily for a seasonal change of scene.

IN A MODERN MINIMALIST WAY

Rudy Calvero and his partner, Will Stewart, spend their busy workweeks in a comfortable home in Los Angeles. Craving a getaway with a completely different vibe, the pair purchased a compact, '60s-era one-story weekend house in Palm Springs, California. Over the course of several years and on a tight budget, they turned it into a cool and crisp getaway, filled with light and decked out in a chic mix of mid-20th-century and contemporary pieces that perfectly suit the style of the house—as well as their need for something fresh and new.

With a little help from designer friend Christian May, Rudy opened the living space to the outdoor pool deck beyond by installing new sliding glass doors. He also replaced ceramic tiles with limestone floors, a richer alternative requiring little maintenance. And he installed a freestanding contemporary fireplace to warm the space. Then he decorated the house himself, relying mostly on secondhand or discount-store finds, to complement a chic yet relaxed indoor/outdoor lifestyle. "Everything was done on a budget," he says. "We wanted the interiors to be comfortable, without worrying about wear and tear. And I mixed pieces from the '50s, '60s and '70s so it doesn't seem like a period piece."

Inside, the house is awash in white surfaces, furnishings and textures shot through with graphic splashes of color. "White feels cool and summery all year round and seems to suit the desert," says Rudy. For the living room, he selected a vintage sofa designed by modernist Milo Baughman and had it reupholstered in white automobile-grade vinyl. "It's very forgiving to guests coming in from the pool or putting their feet up," he notes. A chrome-and-glass cocktail table found on eBay complements the chrome base of the sofa, while a low white table against one wall was a castoff from a friend. A cow-skin rug adds texture and contrasting tones underfoot. In one corner, a bright orange fireplace unit bestows a vertical splash of color.

Owner Rudy Calvero added limestone floors and a fireplace to warm the living space of his Palm Springs home. Reupholstering the vintage sofa in automobile-grade vinyl is a durable, no-fuss solution. The low table against the wall was a castoff from a friend, and the coffee table was an eBay find.

Window Treatment Ideas

An emphasis on more substantial window treatments has begun to re-emerge, and while clean lines prevail in the newest styles, details are back—as are layered fabrics, overscale patterns and color. Restrained yet creative headings, trims and hardware offer extra oomph. The appeal of custom draperies lies not only in the personality and polish they can give a room but also in their ability to offer privacy, insulation and light control. Anything—a ruffled blouse, a shapely chandelier, a stately arch—can be the starting point for a fresh look. And, finished off with distinctive rods, unique tiebacks or contrasting bands of color, creative curtains can play a leading role in enriching the character or even defining the style of any room.

1. SITTING PRETTY "Sunny yet tranquil" was the mood designer Ellen Baron-Goldstein wanted for this gracious sitting room (*left*). She looked to the room's amber and crystal chandelier, creamy Venetian plaster ceiling and glazed taupe strié walls to color cue the silk draperies. Wide vertical stripes in the fabric provide a counterpoint to the horizontal moldings, while deep, soft goblet pleats and a twist rod with fanned finials round out the room's quietly feminine feel.

2. ARCHITECTURAL DETAILS To play up the elegant architecture in her L.A. home (*center*), designer Mary Randelman selected linen Euro-pleated draperies that blend seamlessly with her cream-colored walls and keep the emphasis on the view beyond. Suspended just below the stacked crown molding, the draperies fluidly frame the arched French doors. The linear black wrought-iron rod with self-returns plays off the horizontal door panes to create an eye-catching yet functional treatment.

3. EASY LIVING Little details make a big impact. In this streamlined living room (*right*), designer Keith Baltimore gives French doors a dramatic presence with tan linen floor-length draperies accented by a band of red. By threading a narrow rod hung just below molding height through grommets at the top of the panels and aligning the bottom band with the chair rail, Baltimore creates consistent sight lines around the room.

Tech tips

- **POWER DOWN.** Standby energy accounts for as much as 20 percent of U.S. home utility bills. Monster Cable's GreenPower Outlet HDP 900G helps reduce this waste. The power strip automatically turns off products in standby mode by switching off their outlets when they're not in use. So when you turn off the TV or A/V receiver, supporting equipment including DVD players, game players, subwoofers and other devices shuts off completely as well. When the TV turns back on, a signal is sent to the switched outlets to automatically power on so other equipment is ready to use. 415-840-2000; *monstercable.com*

- **DIM BULBS.** Save 15 percent on the lighting portion of your utility bill just by installing Lutron's Eco-Dim dimmers. They're automatically set at 85% brightness, which extends bulb life by 2 to 3 years. You can lower levels more to further increase the lifespan of the bulb, which translates to even less energy used and more dollars saved. Press the dimmer switch for a few seconds and the light will fade out over 30 seconds to give you time to hop into bed or leave the room. 610-282-3800; *lutron.com*

- **STAY CONNECTED.** The Home Automation Inc. OmniPro II gives you a single source of control for your home's electronic systems. From a PC or a touchscreen inside the home—or from an iPhone around the world—the OmniPro II manages your security system, lights, temperature, audio/video gear, webcams, window shades and water pumps from anywhere you have Internet access. One button sets an Away mode that shuts off all lights, sets back the temperature and arms the security system. Another button can reverse the process and add soft music for your arrival home. Starting price: about $2 per square foot, professionally installed. 504-736-9810; *homeauto.com*

- **KEEP AN EYE ON IT.** Monitor your home from work or vacation with a Panasonic Network Camera. The company's full-motion video cameras—which connect to a home network—can detect motion, heat and sound, and automatically send an e-mail alert for unusual events. They can pan, tilt and zoom for a better view, then store images to the built-in memory. Hook one up to select Panasonic Viera TVs to watch live feed on a dedicated camera channel. 201-348-7000; *panasonic.com*

above Hanging a flat-screen TV frees up floor space and creates a clean, minimalist aesthetic. If you're a Wii enthusiast or you want to feel like you're in a movie theater, hang it high. For a more discreet look that blends in with the surroundings, keep it at eye level. And for the mounted look without the wall damage, the Newkirk from West Elm is great for renters and those of us who can't commit to one furniture arrangement.

above Wooden cabinetry makes modern technology look more at home in a traditional setting. Ballard Designs' Wesley media hutch envelops the monitor, giving it a built-in look.

Case Studies

Case Study 1: Modest Upgrades

Although she'd planned on only a modest upgrade to the kitchen in her 140-year-old home in Saratoga, New York, designer and photo stylist Donna Talley actually wound up making several modest changes over a period of two years, which improved the value of her home and spared her considerable grief had she opted to work on each small project separately. As her contractor was finishing the kitchen job, she realized it would be easier to get him to tackle a small job—like finishing out a niche—while he was working on something bigger. "If I had asked just for a niche, either I'd have paid an exorbitant price or I'd still be waiting," she says.

BEFORE

above Already a pretty focal point in the living room, the fireplace was widened to make room for a functional insert. below Reclaimed brick and mantel trim that harmonizes with the windows blend the newly functional fireplace seamlessly with the style of the old home.

So after completing the kitchen upgrade, her contractor turned his attention to a series of modest living room and dining room upgrades. The first of these small renovations was getting a 140-year-old living room fireplace up and running again with a gas insert. To do so, Donna's contractor had to first widen and deepen the firebox by removing the mantel and a row of brick on each side of the firebox. He then added depth with a layer of old brick installed on the face of the box and crafted a new mantel that mimicked the old. The same reclaimed brick was also used to create a hearth.

Once this project was complete, Donna asked him to add floor-to-ceiling bookshelves to a 72-square-foot room on the second floor. "When I bought the house, the room was used as a nursery, and a crib was about the only bed you could fit in it," she says. Not having a need for a tiny bedroom anymore, Donna wanted to convert the space into a cozy reading area by adding built-in shelves, which she designed with a carpenter to mimic the home's architectural details, and which are painted the same color as the trim. "The depth of the cases shrinks the width of the room by a foot, but the drama created by the wall of books and decorative objects actually makes the room feel bigger as the eye is drawn up to the ceiling," she says.

What Was Done

FIREPLACE UPGRADE

Took off existing mantel and removed 5 inches of brick from each side to create a wider box. Built out the box 7 inches to accommodate depth of gas insert, then constructed new mantel and painted. Added brick hearth and trimmed out in wood molding. Extended gas line to fireplace and connected insert.

> **MATERIALS:** Old brick to match existing; wood for mantel; gas insert; decorative stock molding; paint
> **TIME: 6 DAYS**
> **COST: $2,000**

CUSTOM BOOKCASES

Converted a small bedroom space into a reading nook by adding a wall of built-in shelves. Constructed two 4-foot-wide bookcases to fit side-by-side along 8-foot-wide wall. Framed out cases using molding that matches the existing baseboard and trim. Added pegs and holes for shelves. Painted cases and shelves to match trim to finish built-in look.

> **MATERIALS:** Wood; decorative molding; paint
> **TIME: 2 WEEKS**
> **COST: $1,000**

BEFORE

left A compact bedroom had outlived its purpose as a nursery space and was ready for a new use. above After removing carpet, painting the floorboards and installing floor-to-ceiling bookshelves, the small nursery got new life as a cozy den.

Case Study 2: Making a Livable Room

After spending their first 16 years of marriage in a tiny starter home, Jaimie and John LaMarca moved to a two-story colonial in Glen Head, New York that was built in 1913. "Back in the '70s," says Jaimie, "the house was expanded to include a new garage, a guest room and a guest bath, plus the extra-large room we now call the family room."

With two teenage daughters, the LaMarcas thought it was great to have a 15x20-foot family room where everyone could gather. The problem was that they didn't really know what to do with the space. "It had an ugly stained carpet and vertical blinds, which didn't go with the character of the house at all," Jaimie recalls. "I put a couple of old chairs, the TV and the dog's bed in there, but it was never a comfortable place for us to hang out."

After letting the space languish for more than a year, Jaimie finally put forth the effort to affordably create the space she and her family desired. After removing the ratty carpeting, "we found red oak flooring that we immediately refinished," she says. Once that tough job was tackled, she was ready to decorate. To keep costs down, she reused some of her existing furnishings and added some much-needed new ones. She also chose fabrics and paint colors to complement the palette of a rug—a gift from a family member—which now covers the floor. New easy-to-make Roman shades, which a friend helped to fabricate, add color and pattern and control light. "I'd also imagined the room having a built-in window seat and shelving and leather furniture—costly investments—but I opted for a faux-suede chair and topped an old

above Double doors that close off the computer armoire open flat, out of the way, when the unit is in use. The leatherette side chair is one of a pair that came from Jaimie's dad's office. **top** The new computer armoire has converted one corner of the room into a work area. The club chair and ottoman are covered in a family-friendly, stain-resistant microsuede. **left** The sofa faces the TV at the other side of the room. Beside it, a Roman shade with self-pelmet provides privacy and shields light from the front-facing window. A new floral fabric skirts a round table Jaimie inherited from her grandmother. **below** Two inherited side chairs flank the wooden mini–dry sink.

BEFORE

What They Loved
- The size of the room
- The room's location just off the dining area, where it can easily serve as the central hub of the house
- The large windows, one of which looks out on trees beyond the deck

What They Hated
- The existing carpeting
- The old, ugly vertical blinds on the windows
- A lack of visual warmth
- The room's sparse furnishing, which meant that it went mostly unused

BEFORE

Timeline

Measuring the space, gathering fabric samples and sketching a furniture plan	11 hours
Double-checking furniture and fabric collections on the Internet	2 hours
Painting walls and woodwork	2 days
Shopping for decorative accessories and small pieces of furniture	4 hours
Fabricating table-topper and cushions	2 days
Fabricating and installing window treatments	2 days
Arranging furniture & accessories	2 days
Installing window treatments	4 hours

The Tab

Furniture	$4,385
Fabrics	$1,033
Accessories	$233
Paint for walls and wood trim	$125
Window treatment hardware	$50
Picture hooks	$3
TOTAL	**$5,829**

chest with a cushion and placed it near the window to create the same effects for much less money," she says.

The LaMarcas wanted the room to be multipurpose, so that anyone watching television could coexist with someone else reading a book or using the computer. So the furniture plan includes distinct seating and working areas that don't interrupt the flow of space. On one side of the long room, a new coffee table, an upholstered sofa, a love seat, a chair and ottomans—which serve as footrests, tray tables or extra seating—were arranged to face a new console that holds the TV, DVDs and videotapes. On the other side of the space, a new computer armoire serves as a self-contained home office near the cushion-topped wooden chest in front of a window. Finally, a collection of new cushions and a pretty fabric topper over a recycled side table complement the shades and bring finishing touches to the room.

above A love seat with throw pillows dominates the TV area. The wicker footstool can also serve as a seat or a table. The lamp and table in the corner had belonged to Jaimie's mother.
right The old dog bed and a few pieces of otherwise homeless furniture were randomly placed within the existing room.

DINING ROOMS & EATING NOOKS

LIKE THE LIVING AREAS OF YOUR HOME, DINING
rooms, eating nooks and breakfast bars are essential gathering spaces,
and the furnishings and accents that define them need to support
the process of presenting and serving a meal as well as consuming it.
Whether you're hosting a dinner party in a formal dining area or serving
a casual brunch in a breakfast alcove, ease of access from the kitchen,
ample surfaces for displaying food, and storage for dishes, flatware and
table linens are key.

Comfort is another vital ingredient. Appropriate levels of light and
inviting seating will encourage family and friends to linger and make
any meal more enjoyable. Overhead lighting on dimmers and candles
help set an intimate tone. Soft seat cushions and solid backrests will
ensure that family and friends will feel at ease at the table. And low-
maintenance surfaces—such as glass, polished wood and stone—
make good dining spaces complete.

This dining room is an intimate space, but large
enough to seat 12. The wainscoting, painted with
white semigloss, is an attractive and practical
(easy to wipe off little fingerprints) wall treatment.

Creating Comfortable Dining Spaces

Traditional, modern and every style in between, the dining rooms, eating areas and breakfast nooks shown here offer fresh approaches to fashioning welcoming dining spaces without spending a bundle. Plus, tips on replacing windows will help you enrich the ambience while saving energy and money at the same time.

Creating Family-Friendly Eating Areas

With three young children, Andrea and Chris Roberson wanted their formal dining room, part of a new addition that expanded the square footage in their suburban Washington DC, home, to be attractive without being stuffy, and they wanted it to be easy to maintain, too. Since it opens onto the living area, they covered the lower portion of the walls with 7-foot-high white wainscoting to link the space with the architectural character of the adjoining room. Coated with a semigloss paint, the walls are both elegant and practical (wiping off little fingerprints is a cinch). The walls and ceiling above the wainscoting were painted a bold robin's-egg blue to set the room apart from the more neutral spaces in other parts of their 70-year-old Arts and Crafts–style home.

Keeping it simple here, Andrea decided to forgo a rug under the table and show off the polished oak-plank floors instead. "It's also easier to keep clean," she notes. Accessed by a long, gallery-style hallway, which provides a direct route from the rear mudroom to the main staircase near the front door, the dining room also adjoins the kitchen, a big open

above This family-friendly kitchen is outfitted in warm cherry cabinets and granite countertops. below A 7-foot-long vintage pine farm table is the foundation of a casual, everyday dining area adjacent to the kitchen. Woven chair backs add texture and warmth.

space with warm Shaker-style mocha-stained cherry cabinets and a center island topped with Cashmere Gold granite, which complements a 7-foot-long vintage pine farm table where casual family meals are taken. "I wanted lots of different surfaces for food prep, buffets, eating and doing homework, says Andrea. "We like to have everyone nearby."

Another key to simplifying the family's busy life is lots of clever storage. They rely on a large walk-in pantry to store dry goods, large vases, linens and seldom-used small appliances, while the kitchen island houses pots and pans on one side and the family's good glassware and china on the other.

All About Windows

Most houses will long outlive their original windows. In time, rain and sun take their toll on anything exposed to the weather. But rising energy costs may make the best argument for updating old single-pane sashes.

New windows can be expensive, but you may find you'll get a lot for your money if you opt to completely replace old windows. Technology and design advances mean new windows last longer with less maintenance, while cutting heating and cooling bills dramatically—up to 39 percent for a 2,000-square-foot home, according to the Efficient Windows Collaborative, an industry organization. In addition, the IRS and many local utilities and municipalities offer incentives or credits for installing Energy Star–qualified windows, doors and skylights.

And you won't have to sacrifice style. Today there are many design options to suit most any architectural period and fit almost any size, including familiar single- and double-hung windows, as well as awnings, sliders, casements and fixed transoms.

If your siding, window frames and trim are still in good condition, consider replacing only the window sash—the movable part of the window containing the glass. You'll get many of the same energy advantages you'd get from a new-construction window but at a lower cost and with less disruption.

CONSTRUCTION DETAILS

Traditional wood frames are still widely available, but aluminum-clad, fiberglass, vinyl and aluminum windows are now more common. Frames are part performance and part appearance, and each type has its pros and cons and price range (for details, see the chart on page 42).

Some of the most dramatic advances in window manufacturing are in the glazing, the sandwich of glass, coatings, plastic films and inert gases that together make up the transparent part of the window.

By itself, glass is a very poor insulator and for that reason single-pane windows have all but been replaced by multipane units with two and even three sheets of glass. Manufacturers can inject an inert gas, such as argon or krypton, in the space between the panes to provide a better thermal buffer. Dual-pane, gas-filled windows are now standard in new construction, but in cold-weather regions triple-pane windows may be worth the money.

Manufacturers also apply invisible coatings and films to reduce energy losses even further. Low-emissivity (low-E) coatings on the glass reflect infrared energy, helping to keep warmth inside the house during winter, and reflect heat in summer. High-performance windows use a suspended film of highly transparent plastic between panes of glass to boost thermal efficiency even more.

READ THE FINE PRINT

By using different combinations of coatings and glass, manufacturers can offer windows that are "tuned" for different climates and even for different sides of the house.

How to choose the right one? Start by browsing the government's Energy Star website (*energystar.gov*), which explains its window-rating system and makes recommendations for different parts of the country.

Another source of information is the National Fenestration Rating Council label that's affixed to every new window. Look for two key numbers, the window's "U-value" and its "Solar Heat Gain Coefficient."

The U-value is a measure of how well the window blocks heat transmittance. It's actually the inverse of the more familiar "R-value" used to rate insulation: The lower the U-value, the better job the window will do at stopping heat loss.

The solar heat gain coefficient represents the amount of heat that is transmitted through the glass—the lower the number, the less heat is getting through. If you live where air-conditioning bills are high,

windows with a low coefficient will keep the house cooler. In the snowy north, windows with a high coefficient, especially on the south side of the house, will allow the sun to warm the interior during the winter.

WHAT'S THE DIFFERENCE?

Whether heating or cooling represents the lion's share of your energy consumption, your choice of windows can shave hundreds of dollars off your annual bill and boost indoor comfort while conserving resources.

Exact savings will depend on your climate and the type of window that's installed, but the government's energy office estimates that replacing single-pane windows with Energy Star–qualified windows could reap savings of up to $465 a year. For a better estimate specific to your region, check the Energy Star website.

Window Frame Comparison

MATERIAL	PROS	CONS	COST
Aluminum	■ Low maintenance ■ Low profile is a good fit with contemporary designs	■ Poor thermal insulator, making it suitable for only the mildest climates	■ $165 and up
Vinyl	■ Inexpensive ■ Air chambers in vinyl extrusions provide good thermal insulation. Foam-filled extrusions are even better ■ Very low maintenance and good durability ■ Available with wood interiors for traditional appearance ■ Performs well in salt-water environment	■ Limited color selection ■ Some manufacturers recommend against painting ■ Vinyl interiors may be a turnoff for traditional decors	■ $250 and up
Wood	■ Good natural insulator ■ Easily milled into complex molding profiles ■ Traditional eye appeal, especially on vintage homes ■ Paintable for unlimited color options	■ High maintenance ■ Requires regular painting or staining to prevent rot	■ $320 and up
Fiberglass	■ High strength and high resistance to dents ■ Very low maintenance ■ Won't decay or crack ■ Woodlike appearance will appeal to traditionalists ■ Good thermal performance ■ Shrinks and expands like glass, minimizing seal failures	■ Difficult to form in curved shapes, limiting profile choices ■ Paint must be touched up to preserve appearance	■ $410 and up
Aluminum-Clad	■ Low maintenance ■ Wood interior offers traditional appearance and good insulation ■ Thicker extruded aluminum cladding is highly durable ■ Long-lasting factory-applied paint has broad color selection	■ Paint must be touched up, especially in coastal environments, to prevent corrosion ■ Thinner, roll-formed extrusions not as hardy	■ $430 and up

left A new picture window centers the dining area and overlooks the front yard. Built-in shelves topped by a maple slab to the right of the table create a divider from the front entry. The dining space is open to both the kitchen (to the left) and the living area. below Two panels of an existing window and a partition wall in the original living room were removed to create more symmetry as well as space to accommodate the new kitchen and breakfast nook. The new kitchen stretches the width of the house and now is part of one great room, which includes the living and dining areas. Dark-stained open shelves provide display and storage beneath a countertop of white Carrara marble. French doors (to the left of breakfast nook) open onto a deck. bottom The existing closed-in galley kitchen was cut off from the living spaces by partition walls.

Crafting Clean and Contemporary Spaces

A Parsons-style table is the foundation of these three modern dining spaces—all located on the West Coast and all open to the kitchen in each home. Yet, completely different dining chairs and overhead light fixtures give each a unique stamp of personal style.

MID-CENTURY–INSPIRED CLASSIC

In a Portland, Oregon, split-level home, affordably remodeled for a young family by designer Jessica Helgerson and her architect husband, Yianni Doulis, a set of white leather-upholstered chairs, modeled after Mies Van der Rohe's classic Brno chairs, and a George Nelson–inspired flying saucer pendant give the space a mid-century modern quality. A new picture window affords the dining space a view of the front yard. Framed with full-length creamy linen curtains, the space gets a clean formal touch.

A main problem area in this home was the nearby outmoded kitchen, which the architect and designer reconfigured and redesigned to be compatible with the dining area. They removed the enclosed kitchen to create a great room–style living space. Stretching the width of the house, the kitchen now opens to the combined living and dining areas. "It's one bright and airy space that has a loftlike feeling," the owner says.

Painted wood cabinets and Carrara marble countertops are complemented by stainless steel appliances. There's also a new corner breakfast nook and window seat, and a center island with open shelving for storage and display—all in a black-and-white motif that feels tidy and crisp.

BEFORE

GLAMOROUS AND SLEEK

In his own home in Los Feliz, California, designer Jeff Lewis revamped rooms throughout the house, removing walls to open up spaces to woodsy views. The dining area opens on three sides—to the renovated kitchen, the living room and the second-level deck. The table here is surrounded by high-backed, white-leather swoop-arm chairs and topped with a '50s-era atomic-style light fixture, making the space feel casually glamorous.

right Leather and chrome swoop-arm chairs and an atomic-style pendant fixture lend retro glamour to the refinished vintage Parsons-style table in designer Jeff Lewis's open dining area. The streamlined kitchen was redone with custom-built coffee-colored alder wood cabinetry, sleek nickel pulls and CaesarStone countertops. The backsplash behind the Viking range is Venetian plaster. A kitchen wall was removed to open it up to the dining and living area, and the panoramic views.

CONTEMPORARY COTTAGE

In the Portland, Oregon, home shared by architect Lois Mackenzie and designer Pamela Hill, a whimsical modern country quality prevails in the dining area, where a long, dark wooden table is teamed with white-painted wooden chairs from Ikea and a dramatic chandelier, which once hung in the venerable Benson Hotel in Portland, adds a dramatic playful note overhead. Pamela sprayed the brass fixture white, completely reinventing it. "The fixtures was already hung, so I spent 10 hours sanding and painting on a ladder—I'll never do that again!" she laughs. A Shaker-like ladder from Target leans against one wall in the room and holds table linens. A grommeted curtain from West Elm adds a soft yet crisp touch.

The two women also brightened the space and maximized the room's ocean view, by replacing and enlarging the windows and raising them a foot higher. They also painted all the woodwork white, including wood and beams on the ceiling, which lightened and refreshed the space even more.

The kitchen, which adjoins the relaxed dining area, was completely and cost-effectively overhauled to reflect the spirit of the refreshed space. An island crafted from Ikea cabinets replaced the old peninsula, making the kitchen more open to the dining space and views beyond. To keep the breakfast bar side of the island feeling airy, Philippe Starck's Charles Ghost stools are nearly invisible additions. To link the new kitchen with the color scheme throughout the house, they dressed up one wall of the kitchen with a witty graphic wallpaper called Tres Tintas, which they found at L.A.'s Walnut Wallpaper.

above To give this dining space a relaxed modern country quality, designer Pamela Hill and architect Lois Mackenzie started with a red and white color theme that extends into the adjoining kitchen. White painted wooden chairs around the Parsons-style table lend casual flavor. Painting the ceiling and woodwork white brightens the space, as do new larger windows that let in views and light. left A new low-cost island replaced the old peninsula and opens up the kitchen. The graphic wallpaper adds a lively punch of pattern and eastablishes the color scheme.

Installing an Upholstered Banquette and Adding Architectural Details to Lend Substance and Polish

Designer T. Keller Donovan gave the breakfast nook and adjacent open kitchen of a cookie-cutter Florida spec house an affordable jolt of crisp classic character with a few off-the-shelf architectural elements and shots of cool color. The first step was to add plantation shutters to the windows in the breakfast nook, then anchor the area with a built-in upholstered bench with a crisply pleated skirt. Paired with lattice-back chairs surrounding a round glass-top table, the new built-in banquette adds an extra shot of character and takes advantage of the sunny space afforded by the bay window in the breakfast nook.

In the kitchen, the owners had worked with the builder to select cabinetry with a walnut finish set off with granite countertops and backsplashes of tumbled tile. Donovan enhanced the center island with strip molding set in a series of rectangles "for a more finished look," he says. He also had slipcovers made for the barstools from the same fabric used to upholster the bench in the breakfast nook to link the two eating areas. A valance atop the shuttered window over the sink evens out the sight lines near the top of the cabinets, while a grouping of metal-framed clocks creates a graphic pattern above the cabinets in the otherwise dead space.

BEFORE

left Despite the sunny location, the breakfast nook lacked warmth. Designer T. Keller Donovan layered soft textiles and inviting furnishings to create a cozy space. above A new built-in banquette follows the lines of the bay windows in the breakfast nook. Its upholstery matches the blue strié fabric on the chairs. Plantation shutters are a streamlined, uncluttered solution for light and privacy. A glass-top table keeps the compact space from seeming crowded. The bronze-finish pendant lamp was an affordable find from Pottery Barn.

right A small window, barren backsplash and characterless island base left the kitchen feeling cold. far right Donovan added architectural definition in the adjoining kitchen with molding on the center island. A collection of new metal-framed clocks became an inexpensive art element in the potentially wasted space above the cabinets. A new valance above shutters balances the height of the window over the sink with the cabinets.

BEFORE

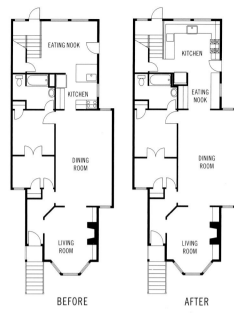

above left The old kitchen and dining area had been added to the home years before, but their awkward configuration made it difficult for the family to function. above right By moving the kitchen to the back, Mann opened the new large space to backyard views.

BEFORE   AFTER

Reconfiguring and Enhancing an Addition to Create an Ample Farmhouse-Style Kitchen and Eating Areas

After their daughters were born, Katie and Joe Morford's 1908 San Francisco home felt like it started to shrink. It had been a compact one-story house with a basement and an unfinished attic space. Although a small kitchen and dining area were added to the back in the '80s, they were inefficient and the entire house was inadequate to serve the growing family's needs. Instead of moving, which Joe and Katie briefly considered, they decided to stay and make their house more family-friendly, working with local architect Andrew Mann of Andrew Mann Architecture to create a new kitchen/dining area that would serve both family and the classes that Katie, who is a professional food writer, teaches occasionally. They also wanted to retain the home's Victorian feel but give it a modern edge.

"We already had a lot of living space, and we wanted a kitchen to match," says Katie. Mann resolved the problem by switching the locations of the kitchen and eating area. The move also allowed him to enlarge the doorway to create an entrance into the room. The old kitchen now houses a breakfast bar, which can serve as a buffet when the family entertains. The new kitchen overlooks the backyard and gives Katie the room she needs to cook family meals and to test recipes.

below The old kitchen, with its green tile counters, was tiny and outdated; the doorway from the dining room directed foot traffic through the main work area. above left Existing windows were retained, but the kitchen, including this new breakfast bar and serving counter leading to the dining room occupy the former kitchen space. The doorway to the dining room was enlarged for better traffic flow and to connect spaces visually.

BEFORE

Case Studies

Case Study 1: Budget-Smart Upgrades

It all started with a kitchen renovation and, more specifically, a stove. That's how designer and photo stylist Donna Talley explains the series of small changes she made to her Saratoga, New York, home over a period of two years. She wanted a larger stove, but there was a pass-through window between the kitchen and dining room that needed to be closed up in order to accommodate the ventilation for the larger appliance. Donna could have simply covered over the opening and moved on, but that would have left a boring blank surface. Instead, she had her contractor drywall only the kitchen side, leaving a recessed box in the dining room. Then, for just $300, she framed the new nook with decorative molding and added an adjustable shelf to accommodate her collection of ironstone.

Realizing it was easier for her contractor to tackle a small job—like finishing out the nook—while he was working on something bigger, Donna asked the same contractor to take on a few more small projects a couple of days later. One of them was to widen the doorway leading from the dining room to the adjacent room that houses her baby grand piano. The new doorway, which replaced a standard 3-foot opening, was modeled on one that connected the dining room to the living room. The result, says Donna, is that she doesn't feel removed from her guests when she entertains them with a song after dinner. "I can see them and they can see me," she says.

above After widening the door frame between the dining area and an adjacent room, Donna was able to create a music room, which serves as an extension of the dining area and allows her to entertain guests with a song.

What Was Done

BUILT-IN DISPLAY NICHE Put drywall over opening of pass-through on kitchen side. Reframed resulting box on dining room side of wall with new, beefier moldings. Added holes and pegs for adjustable shelf. Painted.
> MATERIALS: Sheetrock; wood for shelves; decorative molding; paint
> TIME: 1 day
> COST: $300

DOORWAY ENLARGEMENT Knocked out doorframe of room adjacent to dining room, widened opening and framed with new molding to match the scale and style of nearby opening to the living room. Painted.
> MATERIALS: Wood molding; paint
> TIME: 2 days
> COST: $600

right A new stove in the kitchen meant that the pass-through to the living room had to be closed. opposite Instead of covering over the pass-through on the dining room side, Donna turned it into a display niche for her collection of glass and ceramic pieces.

BEFORE

Case Study 2: Creating Style on a Budget

With two young children and demanding jobs, Leah Bossio, a graphic designer, and her husband, Bob Hugel, a magazine editor, had little time to devote to their 40-year-old house in Maplewood, New Jersey, since they purchased it seven years ago. "We wanted to redo the dining room, but scrapped it when it seemed too big to take on," says Leah.

Over the years, the space became a catchall for everything from toys to an aquarium. The couple loves entertaining and throwing kids' parties, but in this room, doing so wasn't easy. The hand-me-down octagonal table was inadequate, storage was nonexistent and even the old glass chandelier caused problems. "People kept banging into it and pieces would break off," Leah says. Determined to give their dining room polish and make it user-friendly without incurring a ton of expenses, Leah and Bob collaborated with a design editor colleague to help them get the room in shape.

On the plus side, the room was in good condition. So as a first step, they simply painted the walls a more playful shade of blue for a fresher ambience. New window treatments were next, but, with her relaxed family lifestyle, Leah wanted to avoid anything fancy. So their friend designed soft Roman shades using fabric she found online and then enlisted another friend to sew them. The red paisley pattern complements the bright chairs the couple already had. The fabric also ties in with the newly framed artwork—low-cost vintage Japanese postcards the couple picked up in their travels.

As for furnishings, out went the old table, and in came an affordable new model that can be expanded when company comes. Overhead, a cost-effective chandelier takes the place of yesterday's ornate fixture. And with her editor friend's help, Leah also decided on an unfinished sideboard for extra storage. They painted the piece a pale olive hue inside and a handsome khaki on the outside—both variations of a hue pulled from the shade fabric. New hardware gives it a custom look and a sunburst mirror above adds zip. A host of bonus details also adds even more charm and usefulness. A stylish folding screen made from hollow-core doors and painted to match the sideboard lets Leah block off the living room on special occasions. To integrate the desk into the room, a fabric topper enables the piece to double as a serving station. And a new tailored curtain hangs in the doorless passage to the kitchen to hide messy dishes from sight during dinner.

left Lackluster walls and no rug or decorative window treatments left the dining room feeling cold and tired. A desk in the corner also seemed out of place. top right More separation between the kitchen and dining room was needed, so Leah's friend designed an easy-care curtain—mounted on a tension rod—to provide privacy. The curtain's color mimics the dining room wall color for visual unity.

What Leah Loved
- Abundant natural light pouring in from the two windows
- The beautiful wood floor that was in great condition
- The arched passageway between living room and dining room, which allows traffic to flow when there's a big crowd

What Leah Hated
- The fact that so much stuff had piled up in the room, leaving no surface empty
- The hand-me-down table and rickety old glass chandelier
- The way in which the room was underused—especially for its intended purpose

Timeline

Painting the walls	4 hours
Shopping for fabrics	2 hours
Designing the shades, door curtain and fabric topper	4 hours
Sewing the shades, curtain and topper	20 hours
Shopping for furniture, hardware and accessories	16 hours
Priming and painting the sideboard	8 hours
Installing new chandelier and mirror	2 hours
Building and decorating the folding screen	6 hours

The Tab

Unfinished sideboard	$864
Primer, paint and finish	$400
Table	$349
12 yards of canvas fabric	$276
Two Parsons chairs and two slipcovers	$228
Flat-weave rug	$194
Four yards of shade fabric	$160
Wall mirror	$129
Four chairs and pads	$108
Labor for chandelier and mirror installation	$100
18 yards of ribbon trim	$50
Two picture frames	$40
Hinges and hardware	$12
TOTAL:	**$2,910**

BEFORE

above A striped flat-weave rug anchors the refurbished space. Two new easy-on-the-wallet Parsons chairs—covered with washable slipcovers—punctuate the ends of the table. The relaxed shade affords privacy without blocking the sun. A painted sideboard provides much-needed storage and a new iron chandelier lends panache. **right** A dated contemporary table, broken glass light fixture and a hodgepodge of toys left the room looking disjointed.

KITCHENS

WHETHER IT'S LARGE OR SMALL, WARM AND
friendly or industrial and cool, the kitchen is the heart of the home. And, despite the fact that it's filled with appliances and plumbing fixtures, a kitchen is also a very personal space. It's where life-sustaining food is kept, meals are prepared and dishes are cleaned and stored. Some kitchens are all about the cook. Others are family-friendly gathering places. But regardless of its style, a well-designed kitchen gives as much weight to function as to form.

A kitchen in need of an update is a daunting prospect, to be sure. But investing in a kitchen remodel will do more than improve your ability to perform in this vital space. If done conscientiously, it will also increase the value of your home—and save you money in the long-term. With new appliances and plumbing fixtures far more efficient than they were even 10 years ago, upgrading these essential components will enable you to cut your utility bills. And enhancing other aspects of your kitchen, such as its layout, cabinets, floors and countertops doesn't have to mean starting from scratch. There are many money-wise ways to improve this essential room, and any effort to do so is sure to yield both short- and long-term rewards.

Typical of 1930s-era architecture, arched windows and doorways lend grace with softened lines. Designer Kristi Dinner affordably updated this old kitchen by painting existing cabinets a brand new hue and adding new countertops, light fixtures and appliances.

above Particularly in a narrow galley kitchen, care must be taken to keep appliance and cabinet door swings from colliding. The alcove where the range is located was enlarged to fit the appliance. below An inventive use of color takes what had been a nondescript run of boxy cabinets and transforms it into a wall full of lighthearted character. The existing wall cabinets were rejuvenated by cutting away the solid central door panels and tacking up airy squares of chicken wire in their place.

Crafting a Kitchen that Works

Every family and every budget is unique. And kitchen renovations invariably become balancing acts between needs and dreams as well as immediate costs and long-term paybacks. The collection of kitchens in this chapter show how several homeowners and designers took on the challenge of remodeling their kitchens to suit their goals in line with their circumstances. Some were done on a shoestring, some were full-on overhauls, but all involved making decisions that would improve the quality of the owners' lives while reaping the most value from their investments.

Making Budget-Conscious Tradeoffs

When interior designer Kristi Dinner, of Denver's Company kd, suggested a gray and red color scheme as a way of brightening Shelly and Garett Voecks' dated galley kitchen, the young couple hesitated. "We had a hard time visualizing light, bright and airy with those colors," says Shelly, who knew the existing dark wood cabinets, paneled appliances and Mexican tile had to go.

Meanwhile, Dinner not only had to prove her instincts were on target for melding the renovated kitchen with the rest of the charming 1933 Mediterranean-style house, but she had to marry Shelly's aesthetic requirements with Garett's needs as a gourmet cook. "He wanted commercial-grade appliances, and it was obvious that his request was going to eat up a lot of the budget," says the designer, who opened an existing archway as much as possible to make room for a state-of-the-art stove with six burners and a griddle, but kept the remodeled kitchen in the same footprint as the old.

Content to let the stainless steel make the requisite modern statement, Dinner pondered how she could rework the existing cabinets—"They weren't badly constructed, just ugly," she says—into something that would exude Old World charm. "I showed the owners fine European furniture pieces with different layers of paint coming through and applied that same idea to the cabinets," says Dinner. "We started with layers of deep garnet followed by layers of a taupe gray and rubbed it through to get the red on the edges." To prevent the end result from looking like a "sea of wood," Dinner cut out the center raised panel of some of the doors, replaced them with chicken wire, and proceeded to paint the cabinet interiors a garnet red hue to set off the dishes. She also replaced all the knobs and pulls. "There's nothing like fresh paint and hardware to update a space and add value."

For continuity, playful touches of red appear throughout the space. Garnet flecks add zest to the granite countertop, red sliding spice shelves pop on either side of the ovens, red specks perk up the terrazzo tile floor, and dozens of small red square glass tiles catch the eye in the backsplash that surrounds the stove. The intricate pattern is repeated behind the new breakfast counter. "These are all-natural materials that work because they don't look ultra-modern or trendy," says the designer. "Other than the appliances, everything looks like it could be from the 1930s."

above Limiting the visually vibrant mosaic tile to the walls of the cooking alcove not only creates a focal point in the room but keeps the busy pattern in check as well.

Trade Up for Less

Inspired by the success of the "Cash for Clunkers" program in August 2009, the U.S. Department of Energy launched a "Cash for Appliances" program last fall, providing nearly $300 million in stimulus funds from the American Recovery and Reinvestment Act to consumers who purchase new energy-efficient kitchen appliances. To see if you qualify, visit *usgovinfo.about.com.*

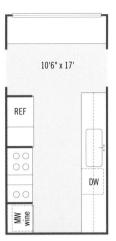

10'6" x 17'

REF

DW

MW wine

left Clustering appliances together makes sense in a small kitchen such as this one. Here, the microwave, range and wine refrigerator are within arm's reach of one another.

1. SNUG FIT A splash of bold color enlivens even the shelves of the well-conceived spice pullout that's tucked conveniently right next to the range.

2. A TOUCH OF SPARKLE A trio of glittering pendant lights adds a surprising contemporary note of shimmer and illuminates the compact dining area.

3. CLEVER HIDEAWAY Counter space in this kitchen is too precious to commit to a bulky microwave, so the appliance is installed at eye level behind a flip-up door.

Opening Up an Empty-Nester Kitchen for Large Gatherings

Having lived in their Mechanicsville, New York, house for 46 years and raising five children there, Mari Ann and Charles Kerls are now empty nesters who both love to cook and entertain for family and friends. But their kitchen was just too small and isolated. "It wasn't easy to move around in the space, which was really annoying during big family dinners," Mari Ann says. And after years of saving for college educations, weddings and family vacations, "it was finally time to spend our money to create the kitchen we always wanted," Charles says.

above A new ceiling, wood floor and island distinguish the Kerlses' new kitchen. Schoolhouse-style pendants are economical off-the-shelf finds.

This was the third time around for the kitchen; two previous renovations involved updates of appliances and finishes within the same footprint. But the space was still stuck in the '70s. Dark cabinets, wood panels, a dropped ceiling and a tight peninsula hemmed it in.

The goal of this makeover was to open up the room and create a better work configuration. The latest design project was a family affair. The Kerlses' daughter Christi, who owns a home-and-garden shop, and her husband, Spencer, then a contractor, collaborated with the couple to map out the project. Here's their recipe for a family-friendly kitchen:

KNOCK DOWN AND OPEN UP. The biggest step was removing several walls to create one large room from what had been an in-kitchen dining area along with a closet-enclosed laundry area. Now the kitchen flows into the adjacent dining room without a partition. A brick chimney hidden within the wall was exposed and serves as an architectural focal point. The new kitchen is a generous 12x24-foot room, with the ceilings raised to 8½ feet. A new window over the sink and a bay window at one end also bring in more light.

DEFINE A FOCAL POINT. The centerpiece of the kitchen is an island with a top measuring 9 feet 8 inches long set atop cabinets and cantilevering at one end for pull-up stool access. "That was about the longest you could cut one continuous piece for the countertop material," Spencer says. All the countertops are engineered quartz with a variegated brown finish. At one end of the island, a bar sink is near the refrigerator to facilitate drink-making or quick wash-ups. Opposite the island, the refrigerator, four-burner stove, microwave, apron sink and dishwasher are set along one wall for efficiency.

CHOOSE CLASSIC SURFACES. For the cabinetry, Mari Ann wanted a clean-lined, traditional feeling. Raised panel doors and crown molding give the cabinets a custom look. The antique finish is the result of a creamy glaze treatment. The drawer pulls and doorknobs have an oil-rubbed bronze finish that matches the look of the faucets. "I wanted the cabinetry to have the patina of age," Mari Ann says.

BUILD IN SMART STORAGE. An appliance garage and slide-out pantry drawers and spice rack are handy features. Near the dining room, a counter is designed as a buffet serving surface, with decorative shelves above displaying creamware pitchers. Several sections of the cabinets feature glass fronts to display additional china.

CREATE CONTRAST. Offering a contrast with the light cabinetry, all the appliances are black. The Energy Star–rated appliances include a combination gas/electric stove and oven with a warming drawer, a microwave/convection oven and a quiet-run dishwasher. Underfoot, the carpeting was replaced with hardwood floors. Six-inch-wide planks of Southern yellow pine were finished with a dark walnut stain. "The kitchen is now our favorite part of the house," Charles says.

right The old kitchen was cramped and dated.

BEFORE

above Display shelves are inset above a serving counter placed near the dining room. The family often uses this spot to display and serve drinks or desserts, Charles says. below The pantry features pullout shelves for convenience. The oil-rubbed bronze door pulls match the nearby faucets.

Spending to Reconfigure and Sell

When interior designer Tineke Triggs and her husband, Will, decided to sell their rental property in San Francisco's Cow Hollow neighborhood, they knew they'd need to renovate both the kitchen and the bath before any buyer would take a second look. They started by revamping the kitchen, which had an awkward configuration, a narrow passage to the dining room, dated cabinets and laminate countertops.

"We wanted to update it but keep the look somewhat traditional," Tineke says of her flat in a 1920s Edwardian-style townhouse. First she shifted the 8x16-foot kitchen's original layout from L-shaped to galley style, for efficiency. She chose sleek, stainless steel appliances and flush inset doors on ebony-stained custom cabinetry. The new oak-plank floor was stained a coffee color to blend in with the existing wood floors in the rest of the home. For a classic touch, Tineke specified smooth Carrara marble countertops.

The designer has grown weary of all-white kitchens. "I try to steer clients toward color," she says. "Warm khaki, or blues and grays. And I prefer clean, bright colors, such as celery." Here, she chose the restrained drama of black, and a stunning ruffles-and-flourishes patterned mosaic for the backsplash. Crisp and classic, the kitchen redo is easy to maneuver in and is sure to stand the test of time.

below left and opposite far right Positioning the stove on the opposite wall allowed Tineke to enlarge the doorway to the dining room, flooding the kitchen with natural light and improving the flow. **below** Tineke's townhouse had a cramped and inefficient kitchen that was begging for professional attention—hers! The old laminate countertops and painted wood cabinets were worn and out of date.

BEFORE

BEFORE

BEFORE

above The original kitchen had an awkwardly placed stove and narrow passage to the dining room. below The new galley plan has plenty of elbow room, better flow—plus a lot more style.

AFTER

left A custom mosaic backsplash over the range is the focal point of the kitchen. Tineke designed the exuberant pattern using Carrara marble tiles.

left "Sunlight floods the banquette area in the morning, and it just lights up the whole house now," says architect Erica Broberg Smith. In addition to the seating area—created out of borrowed garage space—the new kitchen has a large island that can seat four. below Because the previous kitchen was in good shape, the homeowner was able to donate cabinetry and appliances to a charitable organization. Its relatively small size and darker cabinets prompted the remodeling.

BEFORE

Borrowing Space to Expand a Small Kitchen—and Adding Personality

As kitchens go, this one's previous state, with granite countertops and stainless appliances, wasn't all bad. But it didn't reflect the owner, says architect Erica Broberg Smith. "A kitchen tells you a lot about a person," she says. "This homeowner is casual and friendly, but she always wears a crisp, starched white shirt, and the new kitchen is neat and detailed just like she is."

Smith's goal for the kitchen in this second home in the Hamptons was to create an elegant space with a touch of femininity. Although it is a classic white kitchen, elements such as the built-in banquette, citrus-colored walls and vintage pendant lights add personality.

To gain the space for the kitchen's new features, Smith borrowed about four feet from an adjacent garage, which still left room to park a car. An existing laundry space was relocated upstairs closer to bedrooms to yield even more space. The kitchen now has room for a large, mahogany-topped island, built-in breakfront cabinet and seating area that opens to a deck.

The architect worked with her husband, Scott Smith, whose cabinetry company, Smith River Kitchens, is particularly attuned to architectural details. They chose inset

above "The legs on an island can change the look of a kitchen," says Smith. The carved legs here are more formal, setting the tone for a kitchen with traditional elements. The mahogany countertop also has a graceful edge.

What Was Done

- **BORROWED** four feet from the adjacent garage for a built-in sitting area and tucked-away desk.
- **GUTTED** existing kitchen to create a vintage-looking white kitchen, full of upscale details.
- **ADDED** living room–look features such as a coffered ceiling, built-in hutch and arched doorways.
- **INSTALLED** casement windows around the room to bring in natural light.

cabinet doors, which she says is a better fit for historically influenced American kitchens (as opposed to overlay doors, which have more of a European look). Calcutta marble countertops and crackled subway tile as backsplash add to the clean feeling.

Smith notes several other features that elevate this kitchen to something special: a coffered ceiling and arched doorways; the furniturelike glass-front cabinet that stores the homeowner's dishes and glassware; and refinished ebony floors, which create a nice contrast to the cream-colored cabinets. "I can say it's my favorite kitchen I've designed yet," says Smith. "The homeowner really took details to the next level."

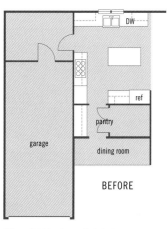

BEFORE

The old kitchen didn't have an eat-in area, and the island could only accommodate two stools.

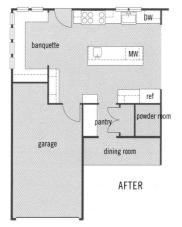

AFTER

After gaining space from the garage, the new kitchen has a back wall full of casement windows to brighten things up.

right The refrigerator in the previous kitchen impeded the primary circulation path. **far right** The refrigerator is now located away from kitchen traffic, with covered panels to continue the furniture look. Although the countertops are marble, the architect chose a slab with minimal veining for a more understated appearance. The cozy banquette around the corner sports Sunbrella fabric on the cushions as a practical touch.

BEFORE

BEFORE

left Among the many green elements in this welcoming, east-facing kitchen is sunlight itself. Raising the ceiling and removing a former wall dividing the kitchen from the family room made the space feel much larger. So did containing countertop clutter in well-planned cabinets and garages for bulky items. above A smaller window in the original kitchen was replaced by a grand one, 10 feet long, and new skylights. The backsplash is now the same coral-red granite as the countertops. below In this family of four, both parents like to cook but neither likes countertop clutter. The blender parks in a deep appliance garage whose door swings up. Another is at the opposite end of the long counter.

Making It Bright, Efficient, and Eco- and Family-Friendly, Too

When Kristin Kuntz-Duriseti and her husband, Ram, an emergency-room physician, set out to renovate their 1950s ranch-style house in Menlo Park, California, the outdated and cramped kitchen needed some TLC—and some corrective surgery. The new, improved version is smart, symmetrical and classically clean in layout, and hyper-efficient, with a place for everything, and everything in its place.

Because of their commitment to living an environmentally conscious life, the Durisetis chose to work with Scott Martin, a San Francisco designer who shares the couple's passion for earth-friendly materials and energy-saving design. And so their kitchen's beauty is more than skin deep.

The space had a "chopped-up layout," Kristin says. First, they took down walls to open it up to the family room, removed a built-in nook, raised the ceiling to the rafters, punched in a pair of skylights and centered a 10-foot-wide window over the sink countertop.

With its bad bones corrected, the kitchen was now ready for detailed treatments. Although now essentially still the same size as the original, the 12x17-foot room feels much larger with the addition of all that symmetry and light. And so there's room for a

What Was Done

- **REMOVED** a 1950s-era wall that cut the room in two, in order to open the kitchen to the family room.
- **RAISED** the ceiling to the rafters to create an airy, spacious feeling in the one-story house.
- **CENTERED** the flow of family activity around a versatile cooktop island, and installed an in-counter retracting downdraft vent to preserve the open feeling of the space.
- **REPURPOSED** wood to make the oak floors and built cabinets with wood from managed forests.
- **SAVED** energy with a microwave/convection oven, fluorescent lights and new water heating system.
- **INSTALLED** solar panels on the roof to self-generate a portion of the family's energy supply.

BEFORE

Walled off from the family room, the old kitchen was both lonely and inefficient.

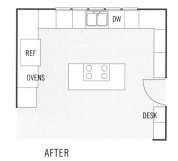

AFTER

When an island replaced the wall, the family gained a spacious place for meals and after-school chats.

above right Hidden treasures of the new kitchen include a compact workstation tucked in a cabinet. Doors swing back, and the wood shelf slides out.
right How to vent a stovetop without an overhead hood that would block sight lines? The answer is a 10-inch downdraft vent that rises from the counter when needed.

new island where the couple's young children can gather with Mom and Dad. "The countertop's 18-inch overhang was made deep enough for my husband's knees," says Kristin. The cooktop is centered there, and rather than spoil the clean sight lines and garden views, Martin suggested an unobtrusive, 10-inch retractable down vent system that tucks away when not in use.

To eliminate off-gassing of volatile organic compounds (VOCs), the cabinet cases contain no formaldahyde. The floor is reclaimed red oak. Only water-based paints were used. On-demand instant water-heating systems deliver warm water for dishes and nearly boiling water for tea, without the need to heat resting water.

Many amenities are neatly out of sight. The free-standing fridge now appears built in, framed by 27-inch-deep cabinets for bulk storage, and flanked by wall-mounted ovens. There are large utility cupboards to hold the big stuff like a rice maker and food processor, roll-out bins for sorting recyclables, and pull-out laptop stations.

Lending Sophistication to a Country-Style Kitchen

Connecticut and country style go together like eggs and bacon, but when Katie and David Barker added a kitchen wing to their multilevel 1950s New England Shingle-style home in Darien, they mixed in some city sophistication.

The addition, which includes an eat-in kitchen, desk area, mudroom and butler's pantry, is bathed in a classy palette of white, black and espresso, while a host of metal finishes provides additional layers of refinement. The white New England–style cabinets are adorned with sleek polished-nickel hardware. Above the stainless steel stove is a brushed stainless hood with a wide rim and straps of polished chrome. And the door panels of the corner cabinets feature a diamond-pattern double-wire mesh made of polished chrome.

"I call it New England with Park Avenue chill," says kitchen designer Christine Donner, whose eponymous design firm is based in nearby New Canaan. "It has just the right amount of bling."

Other key features play off the traditional with high style. The farmhouse sink, for instance, has a fluted apron. The backsplash, covered with mini–subway tiles, has a herringbone pattern, and the vintage-style crystal pendant light fixtures are trimmed in polished nickel.

opposite, top A hefty refrigerator is easily accessible to everyone. The cook can remove fresh ingredients and place them on the island opposite, and hungry passersby can grab a snack or a beverage without invading the primary work area. Thanks to custom panels, the appliance blends in with the cabinets. opposite, bottom The dark walnut island is a workhorse not only from the standpoint of everyday kitchen duties but also from a design perspective. Its dark color contrasts with the white cabinets and backsplashes, providing a visual anchor. The finish also acts as a transition from the cabinets to the Brazilian walnut floor. right A brief gap in the base cabinets becomes an open, pull-out towel bar. Those particularly sensitive to clutter will appreciate having towels stashed away but still easy to reach.

The 375-square-foot kitchen's focal point is the dark walnut island, which echoes the Brazilian walnut floor. Surrounding the island is a powerful perimeter of cooking, storage and food-prep areas. "The marble countertop—Calacatta gold—has a border that is a double thickness that gives it prominence," Donner says. "And the sink in it that faces the range makes it particularly convenient for cooking and filling pots."

The kitchen works as beautifully as it looks. Katie is particularly fond of the high-speed oven, which Donner considers a must-have item for every makeover. "It only takes 20 minutes to cook a raw chicken to crispy," Katie says.

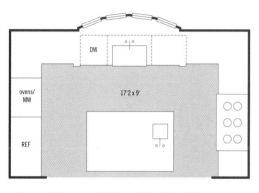

above The practical benefits of the island are apparent when looking at the floor plan. The island acts as a bridge—uniting the refrigerator, range and primary sink—and as a barrier to buffer traffic into the cooking area.

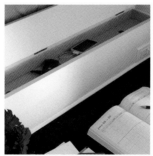

top An understated desk area was crafted from the same cabinets used to outfit the kitchen proper. center Tucked into the desk area is a charging station for cell phones and digital music players—a great touch for this high-traffic space. right The seamless integration of laid-back and modern is amply exhibited here. Sharp, bright metal hardware jazzes up no-nonsense cabinet doors, and a fluted front adds character to the farmhouse sink. A bowed window ushers in the sun.

Surface Strategies

Nothing does more to define the character of a kitchen than its surfaces—flooring, cabinet materials, countertops and backsplashes. With the following, three designers show how surfaces can shape different kitchens with very distinctive flavors.

ECO-FRIENDLY ELEMENTS

Designer Vasi Ypsilantis, CKD, from the Breakfast Room in Manhasset, New York, chose eco-friendly elements to shape this upbeat, healthy hub in Long Island, New York. She coated walls with low-VOC paint in a spring fern hue, topped floors with long-wearing bamboo, and fashioned counters from pearly natural quartz. The sleek cabinets—unpredictable in an old house—look like teak but have a melamine finish. "They emit fewer chemicals into the air," Ypsilantis explains. In tune with her environmentally friendly theme, she also laid painted cement tiles instead of a rug beneath the stunning table that doubles as an island. "The steel table was my starting point," says Ypsilantis. "I envisioned a contrast of old and new along with a blend of textures to build interest."

Ypsilantis' innovative recipe of multiple eco-friendly surfaces and materials packs a visual wallop. Here's how:

GLASS-FRONTED CABINETS foster airiness, while chunkier wood cabinets—hoisting sinks and cooktop—give visual weight.

TEXTURED ELEMENTS like rough backsplash stone and woven-grass shades contrast with smooth surfaces, such as steel and glass, to enrich the look.

CEMENT TILES (cool) in a wood floor (warm) are yin and yang—complementary opposites.

ACCESSORIES WITH TACTILE APPEAL—wooden bowls, straw baskets, grass bouquets—increase warmth.

above The cement floor tiles were air-dried to conserve energy. Set flush with the bamboo floor, the painted tiles absorb heat and resist spills and splatters. above right Pristine woodwork highlights the architecture, while zero-VOC paint imparts a soothing tone. The base cabinet is a recycled vanity. right Ypsilantis paneled an existing 9x4-foot ventilation hood and married a backsplash of riff-cut stone with a Silestone quartz cooking station.

MODERN MIX

Erinn Valencich—designer, author and popular HGTV personality—turned up the volume when it came to remodeling the kitchen in her 1930s house in Hollywood Hills, California. To expand the room's size, the designer gutted the existing galley and back porch, forging one large space. Out went an old window over the sink. In came a vinyl slider with beveled glass. Then for a modern aesthetic, down went a brushed-look porcelain tile floor—punctuated by sparkling aluminum accents. The designer also coupled light and dark custom cabinetry, which she dressed with showy Lucite hardware. Easy-care counters keep company with a glass tile backsplash. And a striking see-though glass hood over the range cooks up a fresh sense of openness. The revamped kitchen also increased her return on her investment in the house when she sold it a year later.

Colors and materials energize this contemporary kitchen. Here's how:
ALUMINUM ACCENTS ensure a glimmering glow at floor level no matter what the hour.
FROSTY COUNTERTOPS—a super foil to dark-stained cabinets— have a clean, modern demeanor.
14-INCH CYLINDRICAL LUCITE PULLS from Atlas Homewares inject unexpected bling.
GLASS TILE enhances the light.
SHIMMERY STAINLESS APPLIANCES flaunt an industrial attitude.

top left "When you lead a busy life, you don't have time to babysit your counters," claims Valencich. "Durable CaesarStone is one of my favorite materials." White-painted cabinets flanking the sink create an airy feel, while ebony-stained cabinets set off shiny appliances. top right An ordinary hood? Too cumbersome. Slick glass—both hood and tile—juxtaposed with steel is a savvy union. With efficiency in mind, Valencich allowed plenty of room for handy landing pads on either side of her pro-style range. above Made of CaesarStone, the convenient breakfast bar doubles as a party station. The artful backsplash is made up of glass and decorative tiles from Ann Sacks. Metal stools slide under the counter, out of the way.

TRADITION WITH A TWIST

Since many of today's kitchens incorporate cooking, dining and living, according to Connecticut-based interior designer Christopher Peacock, "it's important to choose materials with as much design integrity and interest as you'd find in the rest of the house." The British-born designer applied this line of thinking to a kitchen he designed in New York. Recalling lofty kitchens found in English schools, he began with a host of stunning cabinetry—some with a hand-brushed creamy finish and some made of honey-colored quarter-sawn oak. Marble countertops and a mosaic backsplash are utilitarian and beautiful, too. But it's the 21st-century additions that quicken the tempo. Replete with high-performing stainless appliances, silver-leaf tiles and nickel-adorned lights, this kitchen brings past and present beautifully together. Final touch? A pumpkin-toned ceiling—like a glowing sunset sky—ensures a welcoming ambience around the clock.

Christopher Peacock's cabinetry—all from his Refectory collection—proves beauty and high performance meld wonderfully together. Here's how:
IN KEEPING WITH THE ROOM'S SIZE, furniturelike cabinets zoom to ceiling height, creating bountiful storage.
POLISHED NICKEL CUSTOM HARDWARE— also designed by Peacock—combines long-lasting durability with glamour.
DELUXE ORGANIZATIONAL AIDS, such as a two-layer cutlery drawer and steel bins for flour and pasta, are a busy chef's helpers. Automatic interior pantry lights put an end to rummaging.
DEEP DRAWERS house even the most cumbersome pots and roasting pans.

above The hefty oak island is topped with honed marble (polished would look too new) and includes a walnut chopping block. A stainless steel backsplash and a surround of silver-leafed tiles showcase two ranges. right With roller latches and strap hinges, the pantry recalls an old-fashioned icebox. Nickel hardware adorns the painted cabinetry. The oak counter unifies this part of the room. below A marble tile backsplash complements the counters. The serene blend of colors provides an ideal counterpoint to modern steel.

A Word on Flooring

According to the World Floor Covering Association, research shows that the first two areas of a home that potential buyers often look at are the kitchen and the bathrooms. New floors in these rooms can help seal the deal by making a powerful first impression.

Flooring needn't be expensive to add value. Kitchen floors can be patterned with inexpensive tiles for a customized effect. And if you do decide new upgraded floors are in order, your kitchen and bathrooms usually do not consume much square footage, which means your investments in actual flooring product is typically relatively small—which translates into big impact for little cost.

"Money invested to upgrade replacement floor covering, particularly in kitchens and baths, prior to reselling a house can be expected to return substantially more than 100 percent of the cost of renovation," said Christopher Davis, President and Chief Executive Officer of the WFCA. "For example, if homeowners invest $5,000 to replace worn-out floor coverings and then list their home on the market, they should factor in an extra $10,000 to $15,000 on the selling price."

When it's time to buy floors, the World Floor Covering Association's website offers a searchable database of reputable WFCA retail members across the country. All users need to do is enter their zip code to receive a list of suppliers in their area. The WFCA's website also offers detailed information about all types of flooring as well as answers to the most common floor covering questions. An overview of each flooring category provides the pros and cons, a product catalog, manufacturing details, varieties and styles available, things to consider before purchase and how to prepare for installation. For more information, visit *wfca.org*.

For more information on flooring, see the side bar on page 114 in Chapter 5.

Get Cash for Appliances

Save on fuel costs and get a rebate from the government for replacing old appliances with new energy-efficient models. A $300 million "Cash for Appliances" Program launched in the fall of 2009 and funded under the American Recovery and Reinvestment Act for state-run rebate programs will offer rebates of $50 to $200 on the purchase of high-efficiency or Energy Star–rated household appliances.

According to the Department of Energy, states will have the flexibility to select which residential Energy Star–qualified appliances to include in their programs and the individual rebate amount for each appliance, but qualified appliance categories eligible for rebates include: central air conditioners, heat pumps (air source and geothermal), boilers, furnaces (oil and gas), room air conditioners, washing machines, dishwashers, freezers, refrigerators and water heaters.

Unlike the popular Cash for Clunkers program designed to boost the auto industry, purchasers participating in the Cash for Appliances program do not need to turn in their old appliances; they only need to purchase an appliance with the Energy Star seal. The energy savings of the Energy Star appliances can offer a huge savings on your utility bills. Replacing an older refrigerator from the 1970s with an Energy Star appliance under the program, for example, could cut over $200 from your utility bill each year, and replacing a refrigerator from the '80s could cut over $100. Replacing washing machines built before 1998 could save you over $135 a year in addition to saving 17 gallons of water per load. Replacing a dishwasher that was built before 1994 could yield a savings of about $30 per year in energy costs. For more information, visit *energystar.gov* or visit the National Kitchen & Bath Association's website at *nkba.org*.

Money-Wise, Eco-Friendly Tips

- **MAKE THE UPGRADE.** Running an old appliance (anything more than 10 years old) uses more energy, and consequently costs more, than operating a current model. When shopping for replacements, a little homework can maximize energy savings. Over its lifetime, an Energy Star–rated washing machine can save $550 in energy bills versus a standard model, according to the federal government. Similar savings apply to refrigerators and dishwashers. Start at *energystar.gov*, and compare EnergyGuide labels, which are affixed to every appliance sold in the U.S.
- **DON'T RINSE.** If you have a dishwasher, prerinsing dishes in the sink is a sin. It wastes hot water, energy and precious free time performing a task your dishwasher is just going to repeat. Just scrape off large pieces of food, load up the dishwasher and let it rip. Years ago, dishwashers averaged about nine gallons per load. Nowadays, typical models average six gallons per cycle, and Energy Star units come in at four gallons.
- **LOSE THE TANKS.** Standard water heaters keep heated water in a tank. If that water is unused, it just sits there, and if the temperature drops, the appliance will warm the same water again. This waste of energy doesn't occur with tankless water heaters. Instead, these compact units deliver hot water on demand and virtually endlessly. They cost more than tank versions, but a $300 federal tax credit for qualified models largely offsets the price difference, and you can expect a savings of about $100 or more per year in water-heating costs versus a tank unit.

Shopping for Ranges

Most of us can put together dinner on a basic four-burner range costing well under $400. But if the wow factor is a priority, a $40,000 La Cornue range might be just the ticket. Between these extremes are dozens of options using gas, electricity, even electromagnetic induction to help cooks turn out a perfect soufflé, white sauce or roast. If you're ready to replace or upgrade your stove, here's what you need to know.

KNOW THE STYLES

Ranges come in three basic styles: freestanding, slide-in and drop-in. Freestanding ranges have finished sides so they can be placed at the end of a counter or even stand alone. Slide-ins, which lack finished side and back panels, are designed to go between cabinets. Drop-ins are supported by a cabinet, which gives them a more built-in look but eliminates the bottom drawer.

CHOOSE YOUR FUEL

The most basic question is whether it will run on gas, electricity or both (dual fuel). Most cooks prefer gas for its precision, but your choice may depend on what's available where you live.

Electric ranges require a dedicated, high-amp circuit, but running new wire is less expensive and less intrusive than adding a gas line. In areas where natural gas is not available, a propane tank is required, which can be an eyesore unless it's hidden from view.

For gas burners, heat output is measured in British thermal units (Btu), electric burners in watts. Although thermal efficiencies aren't exactly the same, 1,000 watts (one kilowatt) equals about 3,400 Btu. The output of electric burners tops out at about 3,000 watts; gas burners go up to 18,000 Btu on some pro-style ranges but typically have an output of 12,000 to 15,000 Btu.

The most basic electric burners are the familiar coils that plug into a socket beneath the cooktop. Smooth-top designs with the heating elements housed beneath a sheet of glass are much easier to keep clean and are increasingly common. Ribbon-style elements, a more recent development for glass-top ranges, come up to full temperature in seconds, much faster than old coil burners.

Many gas ranges now come with sealed burners to prevent spills from seeping below the cooktop, more practical than the open burners found on commercial ranges. Gas-on-glass designs also aid cleanup.

THE INDUCTION DIFFERENCE

Whether the range is fueled by gas or electricity, the burners must get hot to transfer heat to a pan or pot. Induction cooking uses electromagnetic energy to heat the steel or iron pan directly but not the cooktop surface itself. Induction burners have the precision and instant response of gas and, because of greater thermal efficiency, a 3,600-watt burner has the equivalent output of 25,000 Btu. Induction burners are more widely available in separate cooktops.

OVEN OPTIONS

While cooks prefer gas cooktops, bakers often prefer electric ovens. A dual-fuel range offers the versatility of both, but it can cost several hundred dollars more than a single-fuel range.

Convection ovens use a fan to circulate air, which helps keep temperatures even while reducing baking times. In addition to an upper and lower heating element, some makers add a third electric element at the rear of the oven with a fan for more flexibility in baking and roasting.

GE has taken the technology one step further with its Trivection ovens, which combine convection cooking with microwaves to shorten cooking time. GE says a 22-pound turkey will cook in two hours rather than the four hours it would require in a conventional oven.

BELLS AND WHISTLES

As range size increases (average is 30 inches wide, but they can go up to 48 and more for pro-style ranges), so do the options. High-end lines such as Thermador, Viking, Wolf and GE Monogram offer robust construction, stainless steel exteriors and options like double ovens and warming drawers. Cooktops can feature special wok burners and griddles.

Shopping for Countertops

Homeowners shopping for kitchen countertops have more choices than ever before. In addition to a familiar list of old favorites, a new generation of environmentally friendly materials is filtering into the marketplace. Buyers can now choose from nearly a dozen types of material, such as wood, ceramic tile, recycled glass, natural and engineered stone, concrete and even panels made from compressed paper.

If making a decision seems daunting, asking some key questions can narrow the possibilities: How will the surface stand up to the rigors of kitchen life? How much maintenance will it require? How much does it cost? Is it eco-friendly?

While no countertop material is perfect, the possibilities are many.

DAMAGE CONTROL

Countertops get hard use in most kitchens. They're subjected to everything from sharp knives and food spills to hot pots. Few materials are completely immune to damage, but some will fare better than others.

In most cases, manufacturers recommend using a cutting board and not the countertop itself for food preparation. An obvious exception is wood butcher block. If you intend to cut and chop on the wood, end-grain butcher block is a little bit tougher.

Wood is one of a number of countertop materials that can be repaired if it's damaged. Solid surface—a blend of acrylic or polyester resin and mineral fillers—is another. Sold under such brand names as Corian, Swanstone and Avonite, solid surface can be sanded and buffed to repair minor scratches and scorch marks. Ceramic tile can also be repaired, although with more effort, by removing a cracked tile and replacing it with a new one.

Plastic laminate, on the other hand, cannot be repaired. If you scratch it or burn it with a hot pan, you'll have to either live with it or replace it. Natural and engineered stone (a mix of quartz chips and resin) are both extremely durable but equally tough to repair if they chip.

Stainless steel, natural stone, engineered stone, ceramic tile and concrete all are naturally heat resistant, although finishes and sealers used on some of these materials may be damaged by a very hot pan. Laminate, solid surface and wood can also be damaged by high heat. No matter what surface you choose for the rest of the kitchen, consider a heat-resistant material next to the range.

Stains from food and liquids are a common kitchen hazard. Nonporous materials such as plastic laminate, solid surface, stainless steel and engineered stone are highly resistant to stains. Most natural stone, wood and the grout between individual ceramic tiles must be resealed (or waxed and oiled, in the case of butcher block) periodically to prevent stains. Concrete counters and those made with cement are especially susceptible to stains from acidic foods and liquids such as citrus and wine.

EYE ON PRICE

Countertops are available in a very wide range of prices, from $10 or $15 per square foot for very simple tile or laminate installations to well over $100 per square foot for upscale materials like stainless steel, concrete or some types of natural stone.

The style of the countertop also has a big impact on cost. Profiled edges, curves, sink cutouts and anything else that requires extra labor will add to the bill. In general, the simpler the design, the lower the cost.

Strong demand for granite countertops has helped make this material easier to find and less expensive. Ceramic tile and plastic laminate are also widely available and affordable. But other materials—concrete and stainless steel installed by local fabricators, for example—are likely to remain specialty products and therefore more expensive. You won't find many bargains there.

GREEN MARKET

A surge in interest for materials that are "green"—that is, made from recycled or renewable materials—has resulted in a number of new countertop materials.

PaperStone Certified is made from 100-percent post-consumer recycled paper plus a water-based resin, which, the manufacturer says, contains no detectable formaldehyde. It can be sanded and refinished to eliminate minor damage. Richlite also offers a paper countertop made with phenolic resin. Although the paper is not recycled, the manufacturer says the wood pulp is sourced from certified managed forests.

Vetrazzo and IceStone both offer countertop options made from recycled glass, cement and other additives. Vetrazzo contains fly ash, a waste product from coal-burning plants—another green advantage.

Bamboo countertops and matching backsplashes make use of a fast-growing, sustainable member of the grass family. Bamboo is also less expensive than stone, concrete and other high-end materials, and has the warmth of wood.

Smart Storage Solutions

The kitchen is the busiest area in the home and a magnet for clutter. But keeping it organized will allow it to truly hum with efficiency.

Start by giving the space a good cleaning, wiping down the insides of drawers and cabinets. Take a cold, hard look at what you've stored in each space. Are there duplicate gadgets? Spices so dated they've lost their potency? Toss or donate anything you no longer need. Bonus: As you weed out the excess, you may even find long-forgotten treasures pushed to the back of a cupboard.

Before you put anything back, be sure its location makes sense. Store items where you'll need them most: utensils in the prep area, cookware within reach of the stove, tableware close to the dishwasher and ideally, near the dining area too.

Also think about whether the storage you have meets your needs. If mail tends to pile up on a counter, don't fight it. Give it a home—a basket or cubby to neatly corral bills and correspondence. All kinds of accessories and systems are available, from inexpensive drawer dividers to brand-new custom cabinetry.

1. **EASY ADD-ONS** Chrome-coated wire shelves mounted over a range or cooktop bring tools and seasonings to the heart of the meal-prep zone.
2. **ON DISPLAY** Open shelving and sturdy hooks mean you never have to wonder where to find your favorite tools.
3. **CUT CORNERS** Look for revolving and swing-out shelving that make the most of the dead space in corner cabinets.
4. **MIND THE GAP** Here, because a few inches separated drawer units in a corner arrangement near the sink, a vertical gap became a perfect home to slide-out towel bars. A similar narrow space could be equipped to store trays.

Space-Saving Tips

- **USE A GRID SYSTEM.** A more versatile take on Peg-Board, vinyl-covered steel grids fit anywhere—behind a door, above the washer and dryer, on a pantry wall. Hooks and baskets that attach easily are tailored for everyday items.
- **LOOK UNDER THE RAFTERS.** If you've got a knee wall (the short wall beneath the ceiling in finished attics and upstairs rooms), talk to a contractor about installing stock cabinets to amp up storage.
- **CLEAR OUT.** Move everyday flatware into a handsome wooden box or a country crock to free up kitchen drawer space for less-frequently used tools and gadgets. Relocate larger utensils into wall-mounted baskets or bins. A magnetized strip fixed to the side of a cabinet holds knives or spice tins.
- **DO DOUBLE DUTY.** Run shelves across a window or pass-through and display the pretty glassware that's crowding your cabinets.
- **USE SPACE WISELY.** Gain more shelf space by decanting the contents of bulky boxes—cereal, pasta, crackers—into uniform lidded containers. Corral smaller supplies in baskets to keep them from spreading. Sodas and bottled water can slide in and stack sideways on a shelf. Pop staples such as onions and potatoes into bins along the floor.
- **LOOK UP.** Don't forget to make use of the top of the kitchen cabinets. This often forgotten real estate is a super place for holiday dishes and oversize platters. For a livelier statement, parade your collectibles. Colorful pitchers, bowls and cookie jars will boost your decor and stay safely out of reach. In narrow closets or pantries, shelves or wire racks can store plenty of off-season stuff way up and out of the way.
- **DOUBLE YOUR DRAWER SPACE.** Insert a sliding organizer that gives you two levels of accessible storage.
- **RECLAIM THE REAR HALF OF KITCHEN CABINETS.** With easy-to-install roll-out storage baskets or trays in lower cabinets, you can readily access those hard-to-reach spaces. Good for your bathroom and home office, too.

Case Studies

Case Study 1: Making Cosmetic Improvements and Appliance Upgrades

Missy Shorey and her husband, Roy Kime, are busy professionals with hectic schedules. Their gracious Queen Anne–style home in Saratoga Springs, New York, is a well-loved sanctuary. "Unlike many Victorian houses," Missy says, "ours has a more open interior and an abundance of windows." Still, there was one room that stuck out like a sore thumb: the kitchen. Renovated years ago, the space was quintessential 1960s: gold-speckled Formica countertops, dark paneling, tired linoleum and brown appliances.

"We knew if we maintained the original layout, we could manage the fix-up and not spend a lot of money," Missy explains. "When you start moving things around, that's when you blow your budget." Allotting just $10,000 of their savings, the owners enlisted local contractor John Mazzarrella to help them bring their kitchen up to speed. With a formal dining room only steps away, they also decided to make the breakfast area their den for relaxing and watching television instead.

The transformation began with a fresh coat of creamy yellow paint (a color choice that always channels cheer) for the walls and paneling. Next, the cabinets were sanded, primed and painted with a soft white glossy paint. The sun-kissed palette took years off

Timeline

Sanding, priming and painting the cabinets and painting the walls	1 week
Laying the countertops and installing the backsplash	1½ weeks
Removing old linoleum, laying and finishing the fir floor	2½ weeks
Replacing cabinet knobs	3 hours
Swapping old appliances for new and converting from electric to gas	3 days

The Tab

Wood floor	$4,000
Appliances	$3,000
Countertops and backsplash	$2,000
Painting	$800
Stainless sink and faucets	$200
TOTAL	**$10,000**

left A sprinkling of red, including the red-striped rug, rosy flowers and red-and-white linens, introduces a contemporary note. Green plants (a complement to red) give the yellow-and-white scheme garden freshness.

What They Loved
- The kitchen's comfortable size
- The open layout that makes entertaining easier
- The cabinets' well-organized interiors

What They Hated
- The dated gold-speckled countertops that seemed to go on forever
- The dreary ambience that was so unlike the other rooms in the house
- The floor, which had seen better days

the space, brightening and lightening every corner. A new backsplash of low-cost porcelain tile mimics the look of pale stone, adding polish while visually expanding the feeling of the room.

Out went the countertops, too. The owners replaced the old surface with light-hued 12x12-inch granite tiles, which they discovered at a home center for a purse-friendly price of about $8 a square foot. The existing kitchen included two sinks. Rather than go to the expense of removing one and adding additional tile, the couple opted to stick to their nothing-moves plan and designate the second one a bar sink. The only construction entailed widening the peninsula four inches, a small alteration that Missy says "makes a world of difference."

With all that work completed and funds remaining, the owners could splurge on the features they wanted most—a honey-toned hardwood floor and stainless steel appliances to mimic the refrigerator they had purchased months earlier. Because the refrigerator had a small ding, Missy had been able to negotiate a better price. This time, she nabbed a floor-model dishwasher on sale—and kept the couple's wallet intact.

above Gold-speckled countertops, knotty-pine paneling and an overload of dark cabinets dated this kitchen. Today's version makes a smoother transition to the home's other color-filled rooms. right Instead of replacing the cabinet hardware, the owners decided to keep the existing brushed-brass hinges—all 140 of them!—and purchased new Celtic-style knobs at $1.50 each to match. "The hinges are actually attractive and now they look great," says Missy Shorey. Missy grew up with the handsome bentwood stools flanking the expanded peninsula.

left A sea of worn linoleum and drab walls did little to perk up the setting. Despite providing a surplus of storage, the dark cabinets left the kitchen feeling stodgy and cramped.

Case Study 2: Curing Dated Cabinets and Commandeering Extra Space

When designer Erinn Valencich, owner of OmniArte Design in Los Angeles, a stylist and popular HGTV host, first spied her home, she lost her heart on the spot. The 1950 Sherman Oaks, California, ranch house not only had sweet, diamond-paned windows, it was also in mint condition.

Despite the care, though, the place hollered for 21st-century updating. And, as usual in older homes, the kitchen warranted it most. Here, storage was poorly conceived, counter space was limited and the cabinets and woodwork were knotty pine (trendy back in the day, but not for the clean look Erinn envisioned). "I wanted to double the counter space and open the room to make it lighter and brighter," she explains. "And, of course, I wanted to do it cost-effectively." A tall order, but the creative designer made it happen. Her no-fail recipe for a fab and functional kitchen is as follows:

PARE DOWN AND REGROUP. Instead of replacing the cabinetry, Erinn reorganized and edited. Out went an awkward cabinet looming over a short peninsula countertop—a strategy that now affords a clear view from sink to sunny breakfast area. Two additional cabinets flanking the range were also banished, making way for more counter space and a streamlined vent hood.

BORROW SPACE. The most dramatic step was demolishing the existing wall between the kitchen and back porch. This simple bit of construction enlarged the kitchen's dimensions to 11x24 feet, which afforded room for another counter extension, a microwave and wine fridge. New built-in cabinets were also erected (some with matching vintage-style trim) to boost storage and house trash pull-outs. Alongside, Erinn even managed to stack her washer and dryer behind pantry-like doors!

CHOOSE A CONTEMPORARY PALETTE AND MATERIALS. A favorite sunny wallpaper gave the breakfast area an instant mood change. Then, cueing from the paper, Erinn devised what she dubs

left The original kitchen sported dark wood and a clumsy cabinet arrangement that blocked light, cramped cooking and hindered socialization.

BEFORE

below The endearing wallpaper—"Kanchou" by Brunschwig & Fils—conjures the outdoors. 1x1 accent tiles give interest to the new floor. Pale counters, shiny appliances and cabinets with a high-gloss finish amplify light.

Personal and Practical

- Pull colors from a treasured tea set or a retro tile to concoct a palette. Then look for complementary materials and finishes.
- Incorporate wallpaper or mirror to give a breakfast nook pizzazz.
- Step out of the box by painting cabinets two different colors.
- Include contemporary hardware and offbeat lighting in a traditional setting.
- Hand-paint (Erinn's mother painted the flowering branch), stencil or stamp a lively design on a cabinet or closet door.
- Invest in efficient appliances to save energy costs.
- Adopt a plant. "A $30 orchid lasts for months or years," says Erinn.

above Once the wall between the kitchen and the porch was scrapped, Erinn could extend her counter two feet, plug a wine fridge below and nest a microwave above. Built-in cabinets with frosted glass doors occupy what was the porch's back wall. **below** Surrounded by tile, an original window becomes a focal point. Erinn popped an affordable 2x4-foot skylight above for maximum light. The trough sink is by Rohl. Chrome faucets and hardware lend unity.

"a non-boring scheme" for the cabinets: upper models were painted Dunn-Edwards "Whisper White," while the lower cabs were cloaked in Benjamin Moore's soothing "Gray Wisp." Yesterday's linoleum floor was swapped for durable porcelain tiles. Today, all the countertops are eco-friendly engineered quartz (Zodiaq from DuPont). Cool 1x2-inch glass tiles form a generous backsplash that in some places zooms to ceiling height. The gleaming appliances—a reward for Erinn's penny-saving planning—hail from Electrolux's Icon line.

FOCUS ON DETAILS. Erinn upgraded the cabinets further with sleek chrome hardware. Sophisticated pendants crafted from antique mirrored pieces illuminate sink and table. And cheery flowers are always present. Erinn reserves the prominent display area for keepsakes. The dainty teapots and figurines look as beautiful in her stylish kitchen as they surely did in her grandmother's.

top A beefy cabinet was ripped out to provide room for era-appropriate curved shelves. The new pendant occupies an aged ceiling fan's spot. Laid-back bistro chairs and a glass-top table ensure a casual, breezy tone. **above** Erinn located cooktop and wall oven in the same locale to create a dedicated cooking zone. Landing pads on both sides are handy and safety must-haves. A pull-out board and drawers for pots and pans boost efficiency, too. But it's the sleek hood that delivered the biggest modernity note. "What a difference!" the designer exclaims.

Case Study 3: Getting Help from Family and Friends on Labor and Choosing Modestly Priced Cabinets and Appliances

Kate and Tom Collins were strongly attracted to a three-story brick 1893 colonial in Wilmington, Delaware, but the kitchen almost stopped them from buying the place. "Because it was so dreary, my husband was reluctant to make a commitment," says Kate, "but I have a genetic predisposition to see the potential in old buildings." Kate's father, Selvino Cericola, a contractor specializing in old-house makeovers, encouraged the couple to buy the house, knowing he could save them money by helping them design and manage the actual renovation work.

The 30-year-old kitchen was not workable for Kate, who has three young children and loves to cook and bake. In addition to its dated appliances and cabinets, the kitchen was laid out clumsily. Its too-small work island was also plunked in the middle of the 15x25-foot space, seriously impeding traffic flow.

What Kate Loved
- The abundance of natural light through a 9-foot-wide window
- The room's generous dimensions, which allowed for eat-in space
- The built-in pantry and hutch, which needed no improvement and assured Kate that all of her kitchen storage needs would be met

What Kate Hated
- Its dated 1970s appliances, yellow laminate counters and dark cabinets
- The layout, which included a space-cluttering work island
- The ceiling-mounted fluorescent fixture, which cast shadows and unappealing light throughout the room

left Behind the undermount stainless steel sink and brushed nickel uni-lever faucet is a generous backsplash of 4x4-inch glass tile. below The small work island, plunked in the center of the old kitchen, cluttered the traffic flow without providing very much additional food-prep space.

BEFORE

Timeline

Gutting the kitchen	3 days
Designing layout and choosing cabinets	5 hours
Shopping for appliances, fixtures, lighting, hardware and window treatment	4 hours
Shopping for tile and granite for countertops	3 hours
Repairing, refinishing wood floor	2 days
Installing cabinets, wainscoting and molding	3 days
Doing electrical work	1 day
Bringing in a gas line	2 days
Installing countertops	1 day
Painting	4 days
Installing appliances and plumbing fixtures	5 hours

The Tab

Cabinets	$5,863
Appliances	$4,500
Countertops	$3,658
Carpentry, materials.	$2,900
Lighting, installation	$1,915
Paint, labor	$1,177
Sink, faucet, installation	$938
Backsplash, installation	$725
Refinishing floor	$400
Handles and knobs	$250
Window treatment	$100
TOTAL	**$22,426**

above left In the new kitchen plan, the range and refrigerator exchanged positions, and a new 52-inch peninsula gave Kate additional work space. A pair of pendant lights adds pretty and practical touches to the kitchen, which is flooded with light from undercabinet fixtures. above right Beyond the peninsula is a built-in desk. Divided open shelves above it hold computer supplies. right An oversize refrigerator and bright yellow laminate counters added to the dated, cramped look of Kate and Tom's old kitchen.

So, before Kate and Tom moved in, Kate's dad brought in his crew and gutted the kitchen. Taking layout cues from her dad, Kate decided to switch the placement of the refrigerator and range to raise the new kitchen's efficiency quotient. At his suggestion, she also chose a peninsula instead of an island to create more work and storage space. "The kitchen in our old house was hardly more than galley space," says Kate. "Storage was so limited that I had to keep my pots in another room."

Kate brightened the space by replacing dark wood cabinets with modestly priced traditional-style white laminate ones. She also removed the room's single fluorescent ceiling fixture and had recessed ceiling lights, undercabinet task lighting and two Art Deco–style pendants installed instead. New mid-priced stainless steel appliances add contemporary style and function and bring the space up to date. And since the couple was able to save on design and construction, they could splurge a bit on granite counters and a marble backsplash. "With my father's help, we saved a lot of money on the design of the space and labor," says Kate. "Thanks to his connections, we also got a 30 percent discount from the cabinet supplier as well as free appliance delivery and hookup."

Case Study 4: Working Within an Existing Footprint & Adding Ready-Made Cabinets

Housemates Gloria Flower and Janet Gifford have numerous interests that take them into the kitchen, among them jam-making and bread-baking. When the disjointed galley space with crumbling cabinets began making tasks difficult, the women knew a remodel was in order.

After recruiting Portland, Oregon–based interior designer Donna DuFresne, the owners set about creating a pretty, practical hub that would complement their 1927 city house—which is "part bungalow, part cape," says Gloria—and not devastate their budget.

To avoid pricey construction costs, DuFresne gutted the room and designed an efficient layout within the existing footprint. White beadboard, creamy yellow walls and affordable ready-made cabinets set the tone for the overall decor. "Yellow cabinets topped my client's wish list, so I searched for them first," DuFresne explains.

A honey-colored beam—purchased from a salvage yard for $125—cleverly serves as a structural support and adds character, while oatmeal-hued granite counters inject subtle warmth. "When stone counters don't have much detailing, they don't cost a fortune," DuFresne claims. Instead, a deep farmhouse sink, a stainless steel range and a gleaming refrigerator/freezer were splurges. A Marmoleum floor and schoolhouse lights give the finished picture a fetching vintage feel. Sweet cafe curtains and antique tole trays lend personality. "Now, our kitchen is wonderful for cooking or just relaxing in with a cup of coffee," adds Gloria.

above Designer Donna DuFresne thoughtfully included deep drawers for supplies. Traditional iron hardware is era-appropriate for the house. The French painting came via the family of the home's other owner, Janet Gifford. right A delicious shade of yellow—Downy Duckling by Miller Paint—makes kitchen walls glow. "Oregon is always rainy," says homeowner Gloria Flower. "But it's never dreary in here." The old window above the sink was revamped. Simple unlined curtains afford privacy without blocking light. Lively dishware and fresh citrus fruit add pops of fun color. A vibrant green topiary ushers the outdoors in. far right A glass-front cabinet allows the owners to showcase favorite dishware and keeps the room looking more open and airy. A combination of carefully choreographed lighting—handsome schoolhouse lamps and fluorescent fixtures installed beneath the upper cabinets—ensures excellent illumination. Cost-effective color touches—a lemon-hued teapot and throw rug—ratchet up the kitchen's charm.

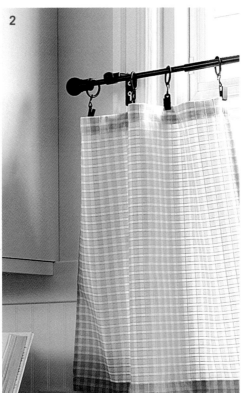

Fast Fix-Ups

Energize your kitchen with these cheery, penny-wise strategies:

1. **MAKE HISTORY.** Arrange a focal point with artful dishes or trays. Here, dark antique tole trays (a friend's gift) also add some sophistication. "Our accent color is black," says Gloria. Congenial linens—the rosy tablecloth speaks to the tray's decoration—provide harmony.

2. **DRESS UP.** Sew curtains for a lackluster window. Include easy-to-open-and-close clip-on rings. Leave the panels unlined to diffuse the light. An inexpensive pull-down shade enriched with snappy trim—ribbon or braid, glued or stitched along the bottom—is a stylish alternative.

3. **STAGE A SHOW.** Bring some zip to the picture with fruit and flowers.

Unexpected containers like kitchen scales, wooden boxes or crocks give fresh-from-the-market vignettes individuality.

4. **ORGANIZE YOUR DAY.** Line a niche with cork, like DuFresne did, to fashion a message center. A wood frame adds polish. Similarly, craft a wine rack for the space atop the fridge. Or, remove a cabinet door and parade hard-to-miss crockery.

5. **TURN ON.** Swap out yesterday's faucet for a new but discounted streamlined fixture. A wall-mounted Danze faucet keeps the owners' countertop uncluttered. "The style marries perfectly with the kitchen's theme," DuFresne says, "and, of course, works beautifully with the farmhouse sink."

BATHROOMS

NO LONGER JUST UTILITARIAN SPACES,
bathrooms today are often spa-like sanctuaries outfitted with any
number of amenities, such as towel warmers, radiant-heat floors,
rain showerheads, Japanese soaking tubs, pre-programmable water
temperature controls and other life-enhancing features.

But even if your bathroom renovation plans are modest, acquainting
yourself with advancements in fixtures and fittings, as well as new
storage products, will enable you to make the most of any investment
you make in this space. Water-conserving low-flow showerheads and
dual-flush toilets or energy-conserving tankless water heaters and light
fixtures, for example, will enable you to create a space that addresses
your basic needs while saving resources and money with lower utility
bills. Updated built-in storage elements, such as vanities with drawer
dividers for hair dryers, brushes or makeup, or louvered doors to
inhibit humidity-induced mildew, can further enhance function while
easing maintenance. Plus, a broader-than-ever selection of materials
and hardware, from river-stone flooring and eco-friendly composite
countertops to brushed nickel faucets and antiqued-bronze tub fillers,
allows for fresh ways to add style and comfort.

The owners of this bath removed walls to
quadruple its size and turn it into a spa-like
retreat. The beamed ceiling gives the remodeled
bath a European feel. The walls, covered with
horizontal 1x8-inch V-grooved boards, evoke early
20th-century styles. The random-length, ¾-inch-
thick planks of Spanish marble on the floor have
a rich leather-like look.

above In the hands of designer Pamela Hill and architect Lois Mackenzie, a small bath became simply luxurious by removing a tub to make room for a 7-foot-long walk-in shower (not shown) and adding Carrara marble floors and sparkling modern sconces.

Creating Baths that Look Good and Perform Well

Creating a bathroom that functions well and looks beautiful can cost a lot or not so much, depending on how you approach it. On the following pages, you'll see how several homeowners and designers wisely invested their renovation dollars to get bathrooms that serve their needs—and enhance the value of their homes. Some made the most of a small room with careful space planning or by commandeering space from an adjoining room, for example. Others bumped out or bumped up space to expand a bath or create a brand-new one. Whether you want to give an existing bath a fresh new look with low-cost surface treatments or create a brand-new bath altogether with a carefully planned addition, the bath redos shown here will help you craft your wish list and create a space that's practical, attractive, comfortable and safe on any budget.

Building an Eco-Friendly Bump-Out to Gain Space and Create a New Bath

In addition to a new kitchen, improved living spaces and enhanced outdoor spaces for entertaining, homeowners Maria and Frank Chiodi also wanted better bathrooms and a larger master suite in the remodel of their 1980s home in East Hampton, New York. With two young daughters, the small master bath and the lack of a second bedroom upstairs hemmed in the family of four. To gain more room in the private quarters on the second level, they worked with LEED-accredited architect Joseph Eisner to bump out the roof line in two attic spaces at either end of the house and create two new bedrooms and baths that are spacious and eco-friendly, too.

The bump-out approach taken to gain space was in itself a conservation strategy, since working within the existing footprint minimized impact on the landscape. One of the bump-outs allowed for an expansion of about 300 square feet, which accommodates the children's bedroom and separate bathroom. The bath is awash in vibrant blue penny-round tile covering the floor, walls and tub surround for a fresh, easy-to-maintain look. An oak slab countertop, which supports a large washbasin, matches oak risers and railings of a new staircase and helps link upstairs spaces with those on the lower level. A low-flow, dual-flush toilet enhances the eco-friendliness of the bathroom, as do an efficient new window, fluorescent lighting and low-VOC paints on the wall.

opposite left In the children's bathroom of a remodeled home in East Hampton, New York, an oak counter supports a sculptural sink. Blue penny-round tiles cover the walls and floor. Where the floor meets the tub surround, the tile is laid to curve up to face the surround as one smooth, sweeping surface. opposite right Designer T. Keller Donovan used a lively blue-and-white pagoda-print wallpaper to lend color and personality to this compact powder room in a Florida spec house at an affordable price.

Adding Personality with Fixtures, Fittings and Finishes

Designer T. Keller Donovan gave a bland cookie-cutter powder room in a builder's spec house a dramatic facelift with a few cosmetic upgrades. New sandy-hued ceramic tiles, used throughout the house, link the room to the other spaces. A classically detailed toilet and pedestal sink establish a traditional tone enhanced by a generous band of baseboard molding. And bold blue-and-white pagoda-print wallpaper gives graphic punch to the small room. "The wallpaper is crisp and fresh, and is an inexpensive solution in a small space," Donovan says.

Refreshing and Reconfiguring a Dated Space

To bring a dreary bath in a 1940s beach house in Portland, Oregon, up to date, designer Pamela Hill and architect Lois Mackenzie started by gutting the compact space, fixing the leaky plumbing and reconfiguring the space plan.

In the original space, the tub ran along one wall with the head of the tub right next to the toilet, and the sink was positioned in the corner against the opposite wall. In the renovated space, the new tub was rotated 90 degrees and now runs the length of a wall brightened by a small window, creating a visually appealing focal point upon entering the room. The sink was moved from the corner of one wall and centered on the opposite wall between the toilet and the tub, allowing easy access into the space.

Applying a fresh take to classic materials, subway tiles were laid vertically to form the shower and tub surround with a built-in niche at one end to hold soaps and brushes. Set against beadboard wainscoting, the new wall-mounted sink brings a contemporary touch to the cottagey look of the new bath, while citrus-hued accents lend cheerful bursts of color.

above The new bath is crisp and classic, textured with beadboard wainscoting and subway tiles, laid vertically, around the tub and shower. right In the original bathroom, the toilet crowded the sink. The vanity lights over the sink were inefficient and unattractive. far right A tidy collection of graphic prints brightens the new bath. Bath linens echo the citrus color theme used throughout the house.

BEFORE

BEFORE

Relocating and Starting Fresh with an Eco-Friendly Design

When asked by a young couple with two young sons to renovate their run-down split-level in Portland, Oregon, one of the biggest problems facing interior designer Jessica Helgerson and her architect husband, Yianni Doulis, was a small, poorly situated master bath. The pair approached the makeover of the bath just as they did other rooms in the house—as a process of removing interior walls and reconfiguring spaces to create clean-lined rooms.

After reworking the public spaces on the lower level, they reconfigured the upstairs floor plan by moving the master bath from the front of the house to the back, where it now overlooks a garden. The new bath also occupies more than twice the space of the original bath, which was converted into a walk-in closet. The designer and architect used a diverse palette of materials and energy-efficient fixtures to give the space a contemporary luxe quality. Saraceno limestone countertops are supported by bathroom cabinets made of a sustainable material engineered from sorghum plants.

The original fixtures in both this bath and a renovated powder room downstairs were replaced by dual-flush toilets for added efficiency. Other eco-friendly steps included using nontoxic or low-VOC paints and finishes, and energy-efficient features like a new water heater, dual-glazed windows and improved insulation.

above left In the renovated powder room, black tile is used as wainscoting beneath a graphic wallpaper print of birds and branches. The countertops are Calacatta marble and the sconce is a custom design. top The existing bath in the master bedroom suite became a walk-in closet, and the bathroom was moved to the other side of house. above Helgerson and Doulis used larger tile cut to 3x12 inches for a custom look as wainscoting around the room and enclosing the lower part of the shower. The tub surround and countertops are Saraceno limestone. The bath opens onto the home office as well as the master bedroom.

left The custom cabinetry has flat-panel doors that give a transitional look. A floor-to-ceiling cabinet with open shelves next to the shower offers easy access to rolled towels and soap. above An awning-style window set in the honed limestone wall of the glass-enclosed shower can be left open even when it rains. The double-size shower area is fitted with a large rain showerhead. opposite, top left A large air-jet tub, surrounded by clean, white-painted millwork, is set next to a pair of double-hung windows and overlooks the garden. opposite, center right The honed limestone countertops evoke the old yet look new. The backsplashes of tumbled green marble have a matte finish that resembles glass. opposite, bottom left The mirror over the sink of one of the bath's two vanities swivels to reveal toiletries stowed in shelf compartments on the reverse side. opposite, bottom right The bath's size was quadrupled to 300 square feet. Its floor plan dovetails with the adjoining bedroom and sitting room/sunroom to create an ultra-comfortable master suite. The suite itself contains a pair of vanities, a separate tub and shower area, a large walk-in closet and a storage closet.

Transforming a Basic Bath into a Gracious Retreat

When architects Todd Pritchett and Craig Dixon redesigned the master bath in their country house, they created a space that was much more than simply a place to shave and shower. By removing walls to quadruple the bath's size and coordinating its floor plan with the adjoining bedroom and sitting room/sunroom, the duo, partners of Atlanta-based Todd Pritchett Design Studio, built a private place that actually functions in tandem with the adjoining spaces as an all-around lounge/living room/dressing room.

The 300-square-foot bath area, which includes an air-jet tub, a pair of vanities, a double-size glass-enclosed shower and a walk-in closet and storage closet, maintains the character of their 1916 European-style Atlanta home while at the same time keeping it up to date with contemporary touches. They also made it cozy by adding stained-wood beams

and a painted-wood ceiling. Convenience, too, was given priority. Custom cabinetry containing lots of drawers reduces clutter, as do the wall-mounted faucets.

The floor plan of the bath is open, but Pritchett and Dixon carved out separate, yet equal, spaces for themselves. Pritchett's vanity overlooks the sunroom and bedroom, while Dixon's is tucked neatly next to the shower. Although the bathroom was planned around existing double-hung windows to retain architectural integrity, the shower's window, which is on the back of the house, was replaced by a smaller awning-style one that can be kept open even in the rain.

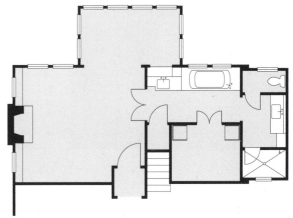

Adding On and Merging Old with New

During its recent remodel, this 18th-century house—one of Nantucket's oldest—proved to need more serious structural work than anticipated. Hired for the project, architects William McGuire and Steve Theroux, of the Nantucket Architecture Group, replaced a rear wing, which was added in the 1990s and housed the owners' cramped bedroom and bath, with a new two-story addition to contain an efficient new master suite.

From the outside, the home's antique persona complements its neighbors. Inside, however, there is a host of contemporary surprises, including the owners' slick new bath. "There weren't any baths in 1769," claims one of the homeowners. "But there's a lot of shared simplicity in colonial and modern architecture."

In keeping with that idea, the new space is like a Shaker chair: beautifully streamlined and functional. Three windows pull in natural light, amplified by a sea of glass tile, mirrored medicine cabinets and an ingenious central glass-walled bathing area. Furthering the airy ambience (rare in a pre-Revolutionary house) as well practicality, half-walls define his-and-hers areas, each with its own sink, toilet and entry.

To introduce the spirit of serenity, interior designer Sandi Holland, of Nantucket House Design, cleverly steered her clients toward a fresh green-and-white combination, while the pristine wood-paneled ceiling and walls tap into both past and present, giving the owners the best of two worlds—a perfect blend of 18th and 21st centuries.

Tech Tip: Temperature-Controlled Tub

Fill the tub at the perfect temperature with just the touch of a button. Moen's ioDigital Roman Tub faucet system lets you customize presets to control temperature and water flow. The system includes an electronic valve that manages hot and cold water by an optional remote control from up to 30 feet away, and a hot water top-off feature. For households with kids, a child lock disables controls and prevents remote operation. $1,390. 440-962-2000; *moen.com*

left A dreary beadboard, limited light and a scrunched vanity demanded a makeover.

BEFORE

left Caps of ⅜-inch-thick tempered glass on the half-walls echo the sinks. A polished chrome faucet and handheld shower are high-profile amenities. Bonus? The tub's location affords a view of trees and sky.
right "We were aiming for transparency," says architect William McGuire. "Glass vanities with integrated sinks are mounted on steel wall brackets so that they appear to float." Set at the windows, the fixtures make the most of natural light.

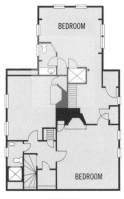

BEFORE

AFTER

top The original wing contained a compact bedroom and an awkward bath. **above** The addition has ample room for a big bedroom and bath awash in personality. **right** "Glass doors on a track roller system close off the shower, while trough grills in the floor serve as drains," explains contractor Devin Remick, of Nantucket Building Company. A frosted shower window fronting the hall lets in light while providing privacy.

Creating an Inviting Retreat in Unfinished Attic Space

After completing a lively kitchen revamp in the century-old Atlanta home she shares with her husband, Mike, homeowner Izzy Semrau turned her attention to converting a lofty, unfinished second-story attic space into a warm and soothing master bathroom.

With walls wrapped in white-painted wainscoting below and coated with chocolate brown paint above, the spacious bathroom presents a restrained palette, but it is packed with good ideas. Working with designer Lisa Grisham of the Atlanta-based remodeling firm Home reBuilders, the owners developed a wish list of bathroom priorities—a separate alcove for a tub, spacious shower made for two, a vanity with two sinks, all in a style that mixes the old architecture with new twists.

The vanity features a slab of the richly patterned marble called Emperador Dark as countertop and backsplash. Two vessel sinks with corresponding mirrors add a cool symmetrical touch. The custom design included a shelf for storage below, although Izzy made sure medicine cabinets were included on the adjacent walls, as well.

A deep soaking tub is given a prominent spot in the room, set in its own alcove and surrounded by windows. The shower is equally spacious and luxurious, made from limestone tiles, glass doors and two large-scale showerheads in an English bronze finish.

Dark ebony floors and generous molding reinforce the feeling of an old house, even though some of the details are modern. Gauzy floor-length curtains and whimsical chandeliers give the space a living room quality. Purchased at a modest price, the affordable accents and off-the-shelf wainscoting helped the owners justify splurging on the materials, fixtures and fittings that make the space feel luxurious.

below With its wainscoting and high ceilings, this master bathroom looks turn-of-the-century even though it's newly remodeled out of attic space. The vanity has deep brown marble countertops and a storage shelf below. Homeowner Izzy Semrau chose a chocolate shade for the walls.

left A wasted unfinished attic was the perfect space to convert into a gracious master bath. Because it was empty, no costly demolition was required.

BEFORE

Replace your hot water heater. That steamy shower can cost you: Water heaters are the third-largest energy users in our homes, after climate control and kitchen appliances. If you're ready to replace your water heater, consider an Energy Star–qualified model. The Department of Energy recently adjusted its rating criteria for the devices, which should save Americans $780 million in utility costs and eliminate 4.2 million tons of carbon dioxide emissions over the next five years. Look for the certification label on three different types of heaters: solar, electric (heat pumps) and gas (including high-performance storage tanks, gas-condensing units and tankless units).

Adding a solar water heater can involve a substantial investment upfront, but that cost is largely offset thanks to lower energy bills, higher property value and lower taxes. The federal government is offering a tax credit of 30 percent of the cost of either a photovoltaic system (for general household electricity) or a solar water heater. This credit is unlimited for photovoltaic systems, but for solar water heaters, it tops out at $2,000. Despite this limitation, a solar water heater costing about $5,000 after the tax credit can pay for itself in five to seven years. Visit *energystar.gov* to choose one that's right for your home.

top left Iron legs on the vanity and around the mirrors provide contrasting texture to the smooth marble and wooden wainscoting. top right Built-in niches on either side of the tub provide extra storage. above left The tub faucet and other hardware have an English bronze finish, which bath designer Lisa Grisham says isn't strictly of the period but still references the past. above right The chandeliers in the bathroom add a little frill. The larger one in the middle and smaller one by the tub aren't even from the same store, but go together in general style. right Draperies in front of the tub lend a romantic touch. The more masculine shower area is upscale in a different way, with varying shades of limestone giving it definition. An acrylic chair is the perfect accessory for the spacious shower.

Adding On to a Master Suite to Make an Old Home Saleable

When interior designer Tineke Triggs and her husband, Will, planned to sell their 1920s Edwardian-style townhouse in San Francisco's Cow Hollow neighborhood, they renovated both the kitchen and the bath to enhance its value and make it saleable. The kitchen redo was practically cosmetic compared to the major construction required to build a new, ground-floor master suite off the back of the house. The designer started by removing a first-floor closet to make way for a stairwell that leads to the formerly unfinished garage, where she built a peaceful bedroom and bathroom suite that opens to a serene backyard garden.

In the 9x6-foot master bath, compact but luxe, Tineke created a spalike atmosphere. There's a double-sink vanity and a walk-in shower, equipped with two rain-style showerhead fixtures. The designer's specialty is mixing materials. For the vanity, she combined walnut wood with a ½-inch-thick, back-painted glass counter and a pair of low-profile white porcelain vessel sinks. The smart design looks super-stylish, with ample storage below that she says "feels really light and open." A matching slatted step-up platform slides out to make the 36-inch-tall vanity and vessel sinks accessible to small children. Hexagonal Carrara marble floor tiles echo the counters in the kitchen. The walls are gray limestone to make the space feel clean and sleek, with the feeling of a Zen garden.

above The walnut vanity is a fine bit of furniture-making, with a coordinating mirrored medicine cabinet above. The slatted platform below smartly slides out, providing sink access for kids who can't yet reach the faucets.

above A large, translucent window in the shower allows diffused sunlight while ensuring privacy. Spalike comforts and amenities include corner shelving, to keep toiletries tidy, and a built-in bench. below The designer fit a whole lot of luxury in a modest 9x6-foot space that was once part of a garage/workshop.

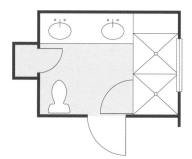

Space-Saving Storage Ideas

A bathroom is a magnet for stuff—toiletries, towels, grooming gear and cleaning supplies. Often, especially in older homes, it's an odd space, carved out of a closet or tucked into an eave, which means there's not a lot of room for cabinetry. Reining in the clutter can help even the smallest bathroom look new. The first step is to clean out and edit: Making a tiny bath with limited storage work efficiently takes discipline as well as planning. Pare down supplies to only what you use regularly, store backup elsewhere and toss anything you don't need. Then examine your space, and steal some of these ideas to make the most of every inch.

- **TAKE ADVANTAGE OF UNUSED WALL SPACE** wherever you find it. Cubbies built under the eaves eke out a little more storage for supplies and a decorative item or two.
- **CORRAL STUFF IN A CORNER.** Two shelves mounted in the corner of the stall shower provide just enough room for soap, sponges, shampoo and conditioner. Large wall hooks beside the shower keep towels at the ready.
- **USE A LEDGE.** A pedestal sink saves space but doesn't leave room for much more than a bar of soap. A shallow ledge topping wainscoting can hold most grooming essentials.
- **CONTAIN THE CLUTTER.** Group all of your products according to how they're used: showering, shaving, makeup application and removal, and hair styling. Keep each collection in its own container and it will be easy to retrieve what you need.
- **ORGANIZE YOUR KIDS.** Assign a different color towel and washcloth to each child. No one will be able to reasonably declare a sibling used his. Carry the theme through to toothbrushes and water cups.
- **MAKE CLEANING CONVENIENT.** If it's easy to keep clean, it will stay organized, too. Stash one complete set of cleaning products in each bathroom. It will be a cinch to disinfect the area when you have a few spare minutes.
- **WASTE NOT.** Make the most of every inch, especially in a small bath. Stack woven baskets in the space under a pedestal sink. Purchase a freestanding unit that straddles the toilet tank and has open shelves or a closed cabinet above. No room for a linen closet? Fresh towels, rolled handsomely, stand up in a basket set on the floor beside the sink.
- **MAKE USE OF THE DOOR.** Streamline the bathroom by making use of wasted space on the back of the door. It's the perfect place to hang a fabric shoe holder that can keep hair dryers, curling irons and spare toiletries out of the way.
- **ADD FUNCTION TO A CABINET.** Try a simple two-level turntable inside your bathroom cabinets. It will give you easy access to lotions, hairspray and more.
- **CHOOSE CLEAR CONTAINERS.** Acrylic caddies let you quickly see everything at a glance, while the individual compartments keep items neat.
- **STRAIGHTEN THE DRAWERS.** Put drawers in order with expandable dividers that organize items of all sizes.
- **REARRANGE THE MEDICINE CABINET.** Group like items together in your cabinets to locate them more easily and keep frequently used items at eye level.
- **USE HOOKS.** Towels on hooks take less space than on horizontal bars—good to know when a bath is shared by more than two people. For less than the cost of a movie with popcorn, you can get a half dozen hooks and line 'em up for duty.
- **CHOOSE A SHOWER CURTAIN** with pockets to hold toiletries and sponges.
- **ADD A SKIRT.** By adding a pretty fabric skirt to a pedestal sink, you instantly create hidden storage for bathroom necessities. It's easy to do with a roll of adhesive hook-and-loop tape.

Case Studies
Case Study 1: Applying Sweat Equity to Upgrade a Powder Room and a Master Bath

When Karen and Brian Colautti-Pine purchased their 1917 house in the Riverdale neighborhood of Toronto, they were drawn to its charm. But the three-bedroom, three-bath home also had problems, having been renovated poorly at various times over the course of its life. So, after purchasing it, the couple slowly transformed it by making budget-smart improvements, room by room. Among their most notable redos are the master bathroom and powder room. The couple saved time and footwork by doing everything at once, and got price deals on plumbing supplies. And since Karen and Brian are not only determined home improvers but talented craftspeople as well, they did the entire renovation themselves over five months.

The 7x10-foot master bath upstairs was the first to be gutted. The couple peeled off the decaying remnants of previous renovations, then carefully removed its porcelain tub, sink and toilet, which were in good enough condition to keep. Next they ripped out worn wall tile, which left some gaps in the walls. And they also tore off layers of old floor tile and linoleum until reaching the original wooden subfloor.

Stripped to the bones, the space was ready for its makeover. The couple began by patching the holes, adding insulation and covering the walls with white beadboard. For a timeless look, Karen chose black-and-white mosaic tiles for the floor, which she and Brian set in a classic diamond pattern. "When we bought the house, the sink and toilet in the master bath were squeezed in under the window," Karen recalls. The

Timeline

Gutting the room, salvaging the toilet, tub and sink	2 days
Removing pipes and reconfiguring plumbing	2 days
Shopping for new fittings, flooring, lighting and accessories	3½ hours
Mounting beadboard panels and installing new millwork	2 days
Putting down new tile flooring	1 day
Patching damaged walls and painting	1 day
Revising the electrical system and installing new light fixtures	4 hours
Installing new and old plumbing fixtures and new fittings	3½ hours
Attaching faux-tin ceiling	3 hours
Hanging curtains	1 hour
Installing medicine cabinet salvaged from downstairs bath	1 hour

The Tab

Plumbing, including new faucets, handles	$537
Beadboard plus all lumber, trim and a new wood door	$232
Accessories	$220
Wiring, electrical equipment, light fixtures	$158
Tile, grout and adhesive	$146
Laminate flooring	$75
Window curtains, shower curtain	$60
Paint	$33
Insulation	$25
Faux tin wallpaper for ceiling	$15
TOTAL	**$1,501**

BEFORE

left During renovation of the master bath, Brian and Karen Colautti-Pine left the tub where it was, but they installed new tile above and around it, and added new shower fittings. They removed the old tile, which covered the floor and ran three-quarters of the way up the walls. The sink and toilet were moved from under the window to the adjacent wall. **above** In the remodeled master bath, a wooden medicine cabinet from the downstairs bath was added and perked up with white paint. Sunlight filters through the curtain that dresses the original window. White fixtures, a white-painted towel rack and shelf, plus the repainted medicine cabinet create a vintage look set against the beadboard walls.

Timeline

Removing old pipes and revising the plumbing	2 days
Installing new window and millwork	1½ days
Gutting the room, salvaging floor tile and toilet	1 day
Installing new and old plumbing fixtures and new fittings	3½ hours
Shopping for new hardware, fabric and accessories	3 hours
Redoing electric system and installing new light fixtures	3 hours
Putting down laminate flooring	2 hours
Patching walls and painting walls and trim	2 hours
Hanging mirror and towel shelf	1 hour
Embellishing and hanging window curtain and tieback	2 hours

The Tab

Plumbing	$400
Lumber and insulation	$349
New door and window	$319
New sink, faucets, accessories	$161
New wiring and lighting	$108
Flooring	$75
Window curtain and trim	$45
Curtain rod and shelf	$25
Wall and trim paint	$18
TOTAL	**$1,500**

couple spaced out these fixtures more sensibly against the wall opposite the tub. They also retained the room's original window, but created new window casing millwork as well as baseboard molding. Finally, they placed a new shower over the tub, put up a crisp white shower curtain, and hung a ready-made window curtain in front of the window.

For Karen and Brian, one of the house's main attractions was its conveniently placed first-floor powder room. This room, like others in the house, had changed much over time. "It was once a pantry," says Karen. Since there were no bedrooms on that level, its shower seemed superfluous, so the couple eliminated it, shrinking the bath to 4x6 feet and adding the bonus square footage to their kitchen remodel. In gutting the bath, they removed its 12x12-inch floor tiles carefully, then reused them in the laundry room. The room's small existing window needed replacement. "But we didn't want to have to replace the header, so we put in a new frosted-glass window that was the same size," says Karen.

Another budget-smart step the couple took to improve the room was to install the same flooring that they used for the kitchen. "It's a laminate that looks like an old wooden barn floor," says Karen. Also, as in the master bath, she and Brian crafted the window casing and baseboard molding—and even built a combination shelf and dowel directly above a new toile tieback curtain. Although the couple purchased a new pedestal sink, mirror, shelf and sconces, they recycled and repositioned the original toilet. Throughout both baths, new faucets and handles freshened up all of the recycled fixtures.

above The old downstairs bath had a corner shower and a vanity that were no longer needed. Both were scrapped; only the toilet, of fairly recent vintage, was reused. right For the powder room, Karen sewed loops and fringe on a curtain panel, then swagged it for a dramatic effect. She positioned it to emphasize the height of the room and make the window appear larger. An old glass doorknob was mounted on the wall so the powder room curtain could tie back beautifully with black cording to the knob.

Case Study 2: Borrowing Attic and Closet Space to Create a Shared Upstairs Bath

After 16 years of middle-of-the-night trips down a steep flight of stairs from their upstairs bedrooms to their home's sole bathroom, Gloria Flower and Janet Gifford knew it was time for a change. Co-owners of a 1927 house in Portland, Oregon, the women had hired Portland-based interior designer Donna DuFresne to remodel their aging kitchen. In the process, they asked her to inspect the unused attic storage space off Gloria's bedroom as a possible location for an upstairs bathroom. To their delight, Donna found a way to convert the space viably—both physically and financially—into a bright bathroom space complete with a shower.

Gloria had a tiny closet in her bedroom that led to a small access door to the attic space. To create the bathroom, DuFresne captured a portion of the unused attic area and combined it with Gloria's closet and a 3x6-foot slice out of Jan's room that became the bathroom's 3x3 shower backed by a 3x3 closet. The bath is entered from Gloria's side through the existing closet door, and a second bathroom door, mirroring Gloria's, opens into the bath from Jan's side. In addition, a pair of new operable skylights not only brings ventilation and light into the room, but also provides the illusion of more height and space. And by running the plumbing upstairs while the kitchen walls were open during its remodel, the designer saved the women a bundle.

Once the space had been shaped, DuFresne applied her talents to finishing out the room with a sense of period-appropriate charm at a reasonable price. Vintage-inspired materials found at inexpensive outlets solved the design dilemma. The designer chose beadboard, 1-inch-square hexagonal floor tiles and 4x4-inch white tiles for the shower stall, which she finished with handsome black quarter-round cap tiles.

above The vintage mirror sits on an easel built into the wall, so that it can be tilted for easy viewing. A pair of vintage sconces was only $20. The wall color adds airiness to the low ceiling space. A ledge provides storage for soaps, a clock and accessories.

Storage space is tucked tidily behind a door on the built-in shelves above the commode. Towels, books and mementos are displayed on the open shelves. A trio of plants happily sits in brilliant pots on the ledge above the beadboard wainscoting, which ties in with the tongue-and-groove ceiling around the skylights. And mirrors—including one on the $29 medicine cabinet from Lowe's, an old $80 vanity mirror above the pedestal sink, and a full-length one set on a recycled vintage door—help to visually enlarge the space and give it a sense of airiness by reflecting the natural and artificial light.

left In an oddly angled area of the bathroom beneath the slanted roofline, designer Donna DuFresne installed built-in shelves, replete with storage, that are trimmed out in a step-down fashion that adds the perfect note of panache.

BEFORE

center left The space for the shower stall, which is shown here in an unfinished state, was "borrowed" from Janet's bedroom. left The shower stall is handsomely finished with white tile, readily available at most outlets. The black trim and cap tiles echo the black hexagonal tiles in the floor. A black-and-white shower curtain lends a soft touch.

The Tab

Construction, lumber build-out, framing closet, skylight work	$14,721
Plumbing	$1,000
Electrical work	$ 800
Tile	$650
Skylights	$600
Toilet & sink	$400
Lighting/fan	$160
Custom-made shower curtain	$80
Vintage mirror	$80
Door	$50
Beadboard	$40
Paint	$40
Medicine cabinet	$29
TOTAL	**$18,650**

BEFORE

left DuFresne used budget-minded materials—hexagonal floor tiles, matching pedestal sink and commode, and beadboard—to create a period-appropriate look. A vintage door was found for $50. A mirror was added with vintage hardware. far left DuFresne carved out space from a tiny closet and an adjacent unused storage area in the attic to create the upstairs bath. The build-out for the bathroom sink is seen here, along with the skylight opening.

Case Study 3: Keeping Plumbing in Existing Locations to Save Money

The rooms of the 1920 Hollywood Hills home that L.A. designer Erinn Valencich purchased a few years ago and later sold at a premium, brimmed with charm—all but the worn and dated baths, that is. A past remodel had left the master bath with an awkward tub/shower unit, a bulky vanity and a stained-glass window that blocked the cheery California light and garden views. And the guest bath, with its clumsy cave-like shower and dingy old linoleum, wasn't any better.

Although the architecture was Spanish in style, the house actually had only a few Mediterranean-flavor interior details. So Erinn, who is also a popular host of various HGTV specials, was free to give the rooms her own contemporary spin. Her goal for these fix-ups, which she tackled before moving in, included making the baths feel more spacious, light-filled and modern. Since she was handling two projects at once, she also wanted to closely monitor costs and be prudent where possible. Keeping all the plumbing in existing locations saved Erinn a bundle. She had enough left over, in fact, to make a real splash with stunning materials and fixtures.

She began by gutting both rooms and devising schemes that amplify the feeling of spaciousness. With her busy schedule, Erinn has little time for soaking. "Showers

below The guest bath's self-rimmed sink is a focal point. According to designer Erinn Valencich, extending the 12x24-inch textured shower tiles along the vanity wall gives the room "more fluidity." The new beveled mirror appears to double the room's size. bottom left An inadequate vanity and a clumsy tub/shower did little for the old master bath.

BEFORE

100 bathrooms

are more sensible for me," she says. So now the 6x10-foot master bath boasts a generous glass shower with a convenient built-in bench. And to conjure a more open feeling, the 7x12-foot guest bath sports a walk-in transparent shower, too. Erinn also designed floating ebony-stained wood vanities to accommodate towels and toiletries. "Without legs, they look airy, not heavy," she says.

To convey freshness and light, she opted for sleek fixtures as well as reflective finishes and fittings. Eye-catching sinks from Kohler's Wading Pool series and sleek brushed-nickel faucets rocket the baths into the present century, while large mirrors visually expand the rooms' dimensions and increase light. Even the toilets, particularly the master's tankless hatbox-style model, are cool and super-efficient!

Touches of texture tone down the modernity with a bit of earthy warmth. For the master shower, Erinn chose a pebble floor and gray and brown bamboo-look wall tile in two different sizes. "I wanted it to look like a rain forest," she says. A soothing CaesarStone countertop and a stone floor—laid in a striking herringbone pattern—heighten the luxe mood. The guest bath also features a heady mix of materials: glazed porcelain tile (Xilo from Artistic Tile) that has the look of rich wood, teamed with a classy gray-and-white wallcovering.

As finishing touches, artful sconces aid grooming and add a glamorous vibe. And so do wallet-friendly prints and faux bouquets. "These are great additions," says Erinn, "as long as they fit proportionally and are never allowed to gather dust."

Low-Maintenance High Style

Designer Erinn Valencich offers these tips on creating a bath that's chic and easy to clean.

- Choose a light palette and use high-gloss paint to make it easier to track and remove grime.
- Opt for engineered quartz countertops for a natural-surface look that's stain- and bacteria-resistant.
- Incorporate seamless tub surrounds—they're easy to wipe down.
- Consider faucet fixtures in finishes such as brushed chrome that will hide water spots and won't corrode.
- Install undermounted sinks to minimize scrubbing.
- Get the look of wood or tile without worrying about warping or water rot by laying attractive laminate flooring.
- Create homes for towels and supplies with integrated closets, cabinets and open shelves.

BEFORE

left With its worn linoleum teamed with pale walls and uninteresting fixtures, yesterday's guest bath was stuck in the past. **right** Chunky geometric hardware dresses up the vanity. The graphic wallcovering links the scene to the outdoors. And since the guest bath seldom gets steamy, a light-diffusing silk shade is a perfect embellishment.

BEDROOMS

THE BEDROOM IS WHERE WE WAKE TO BEGIN EACH day and lay down our head to end it, so it's important to make this vital space a comfort zone that soothes the senses and nourishes the soul. Shaping a bedroom's shell—its walls, windows, ceiling and floor—with character-building elements, such as crown molding and color, curtains and carpet, will go a long way in turning a bare-bones space into an inviting sanctuary. Tactile soft furnishings afford an ideal way to add comfort and, in this most private of spaces, a generous dose of personality, too.

The bed, of course, is the centerpiece of the setting, so be sure to set the tone with one that ideally suits your style. Then build the room around it, with multipurpose pieces such as television armoires with deep drawers for extra bedding, benches that hold blankets and quilts, or night tables with drawers for remote controls and shelves for magazines. Proper lighting is crucial in bedrooms for casting focused light on the pages of an open book at night or for ensuring that socks match in the morning. And ample storage is another essential ingredient. A place for everything—from jewelry and lingerie to shirts and shoes—will ensure a peaceful start and close to your day.

In a guest room enveloped in a pear-green hue, designer Libby Langdon painted an old rattan bed black to coordinate with a black-and-white Chinese-scene toile from Duralee. The elegant linens were bought at a bargain from T.J. Maxx and Linens 'n Things. "If you don't splurge on expensive guest room linens but shop for affordable, stylish coordinates, then you can switch them out every season and not worry about the wear and tear guests might cause."

Inviting Private Spaces

Crafting your own private oasis is often about function as much as it is form. Your dream room may be a low-maintenance space with Zen-like simplicity. Or it may be a plush haven with fine bedding, soft carpet and well-dressed windows. Whether your starting point is a compact space with little wiggle room or a generous space with enough square footage to allow for separate zones for reading in an upholstered chair, writing at a laptop on a desk, watching TV at night or taking tea at a breakfast table in the morning, you can define a space that both responds to your needs and meets your budget. The pages that follow are filled with inspiring bedrooms—master suites, children's rooms and guest spaces—that are as practical as they are attractive. Brimming with ideas to fit any size and suit any style, all are designed for comfort and ease.

Adding a Spacious Master Suite to an Older Home, Then Decorating on a Budget

Brooke and Bryan Crane's first house in Los Angeles—a one-story, two-bedroom cottage originally built in 1926—came with plenty of period charm intact, but it lacked sufficient space for a young couple with a baby on the way. One of their first priorities was to add a spacious master suite that would overlook the home's garden. "I love the cottage look, so we tried to remodel in the spirit of the original house," says Brooke. Investing in the addition didn't leave a huge budget for decorating, but with the help of Brooke's mother, Kitty Bartholomew, a former television host and author known for her decorating wisdom, they were able to make wise color and pattern choices. The lower portions of the bedroom walls are sheathed in a creamy hue, allowing the classic blue-and-white toile covering the headboard, reading chair and night table to stand out. Above a strip of crown molding, which was mounted a foot and a half below the ceiling to create a more intimate sense of scale in the room, the walls and ceiling are painted an airy blue, capping the room with a serene sky-like quality. Recycled hand-me-down pieces and repurposed objects, as well as bargain pieces found on Craigslist and other websites enabled the couple to personalize the space with creature comforts that make the room their favorite in the home.

below Memories abound in a corner of the new master bedroom, where vases used at Brooke and Bryan's wedding reception cluster on the dresser. The blue-and-white lampshade is made from their wedding cake tablecloth. The mirror came home from an estate sale. opposite In the master bedroom, a grandmother's tablecloth of Battenburg lace tops the bedside table. Other old linens were repurposed as lampshades, crowning vases used at the couple's wedding reception, which were converted to lamps. Painted sky-blue, the ceiling is coved, copying the architecture of the living room.

left Jeff Lewis combined two of the five bedrooms in his 1963 house to create a luxurious master suite with a room-size closet and spacious master bath that also takes advantage of views. The master bedroom's minimalist design is reflected in the all-white oil paintings above the bed by Christopher Classen. Seagrass wallcovering adds natural texture, while linens from Restoration Hardware introduce crisp graphic appeal. The ribbed rug from Crate & Barrel grounds the room with earthy warmth. opposite top A self-confessed neat freak, Jeff says his 10x12-foot closet fitted with custom-built cabinets is one of his favorite things about the house. "I feel like I'm in a clothing store—everything is color-coded and organized by type of garment," he says. opposite bottom Combining two bedrooms allowed Jeff to create this luxurious master bath, with a vast limestone shower and volcanic-limestone soaking tub.

Opening Small Rooms to Create a Sense of Expansiveness, Calm and Order in a Masculine Master Suite

In keeping with the approach he took in designing the other rooms in his 1963 house in Los Feliz, California, designer Jeff Lewis took steps to improve his master bedroom in ways that would increase the home's resale value as well as the bedroom's comfort.

With five bedrooms in the house, there were too many small spaces and not enough large ones, so two bedrooms were combined to create a luxurious master suite with a room-size closet and spacious master bath with new windows that also takes advantage of views.

Creating a more open space plan brightened the room, but to warm it, he applied a textured seagrass wallcovering to the walls and added a thick ribbed rug underfoot to ground the space. As in other rooms, clean-lined, minimalist furnishings and accents keep the room feeling orderly and calm, as does the new closet with custom-built cabinets that hide clutter.

Tricks of the Flipper Trade

Designer Jeff Lewis, host of the television program *Flipping Out,* offers these tips for cost-effectively improving the value of your home:

- **ADD MORE SUBSTANTIAL CROWN AND BASEBOARD MOLDING.** "A lot of times I use MDF molding, which is half the price of solid wood but still looks great," he says.
- **ENLARGE OR RAISE DOOR OR WINDOW OPENINGS.** "Raising the doorway heights six inches or widening an opening a foot and a half improves proportions, makes ceilings seem taller and rooms more spacious."
- **UPDATE LIGHT SWITCHES AND OUTLET PLATES.** Swapping out doorknobs and cabinet hardware can also have a major impact. If doors are hollow-core, invest in solid-wood doors for an instant uptick in quality.
- **PAINT WALLS A COLOR OTHER THAN PLAIN WHITE.** It can be a neutral, but it can still be warm and rich, like gray-green, taupe or chocolate brown.

Enriching a Bland Room with Affordable Architectural Upgrades and Finishes, and Lending Personality With Fabrics

COTTAGEY AND SOFT

After upgrading their 1956 house in Tustin, California, with new windows and doors, Sara and Josh Duckett turned their attention to enhancing the interior spaces with cosmetic finish treatments. As in other rooms throughout the house, they refinished the wood floors in a small guest room with a rich dark stain for warmth and drama, then primed and painted walls in the muted neutral hues Sara favors. This room got an extra dose of warmth with the addition of wainscoting painted a soft celadon hue, while smocked sheers on the windows, and gathered dust ruffles and floral duvet covers on the twin beds with upholstered headboards, lend the space a soft, feminine, casual feeling.

right Owner Sara Duckett opted for twin beds in a small guest room so as not to overwhelm the space. Newly refinished floors and simple wainscoting enrich the room with warmth.

TAILORED AND CRISP

Extending the strategy he employed to enrich the other cookie-cutter rooms in a Florida spec house, designer T. Keller Donovan lifted the character of the master bedroom by adding crown molding around the ceiling and plantation shutters to the windows, which help regulate heating and cooling in the Florida climate. To introduce a sense of comfort and crisp flavor, he added a neutral, tightly woven carpet atop the ceramic tile floors and oriental toile and strié fabrics that extend the beachy color scheme used in other spaces. The fabrics' graphic print and color give punch to the serene space awash in textured solids. Tailored touches, like grosgrain ribbon trim on pillows, sharply pleated chair and bed skirts, and white piping on an ottoman and chair cushion, keep the space clean and crisp.

above The rooms had a cookie-cutter quality, completely lacking in architectural detail.
left An oriental toile fabric covers the headboard and dust ruffle in the master bedroom. The chair's blue strié upholstery is a fabric carried over from the kitchen. White piping adds a tailored feeling. Prints depicting Asian costumes add antique style, while the neutral carpeting softens the room. Sand-colored ceramic flooring establishes a flow from room to room. And in this room, a natural-hued rug keeps the look light underfoot.

Space-Saving Tips

■ **STORE ON DISPLAY.** Come up with ways to display pretty things that take up drawer or shelf space so you can make room for less attractive items. Mounting and framing your family photos could free up a couple feet of space eaten up by albums. Display your vintage necklaces on the wall above your bureau to make way for more socks and underwear in your top drawer.

■ **MAKE THE MOST OF DOORS.** Hang up a canvas or plastic shoe bag. Besides shoes, they're great for craft supplies, socks, small toiletries—anything that needs a place to call home.

■ **DON'T IGNORE THE SPACE UNDER YOUR BED.** Get a sturdy cardboard underbed box for a few bucks, or upgrade to shallow plastic bins with wheels and hinged lids.

■ **TAKE CONTROL OF THE INSIDE OF CLOSET DOORS.** Mount a peg rack for neckties and belts. A hanging vinyl shoe bag holds extra shoes or small accessories like scarves and socks.

■ **TURN THE BED INTO A STORAGE SYSTEM.** Substitute shelves for a headboard. Radio, clock, mystery novels? All your must-haves can stay close at hand. Built-in drawers and cabinets around a platform bed store extra bedding or clothes—and leave no room for dust bunnies!

above In a spare and simple bedroom, a space-saving bed with built-in tables came from Ikea. One wall is painted a rich brown-gray for dramatic emphasis. below The bed in this eco-friendly room doubles as a storage unit with built-in drawers in the headboard and under the platform. Pale gray walls, painted with low- or no-VOC paint, complement the bedroom's sleek lines. An old metal dresser was repainted at an auto-body shop.

Easing the Line Between Indoors and Out

BEACHY AND BRIGHT

A master bedroom addition to an 1960s ranch in Southern California, updated by designer Amanda Sandberg, was designed, like other rooms in the house, to have a direct link to the outdoors. Although she tends to keep the color scheme consistent from room to room in the homes she renovates, she changes up the color palette in the bedrooms. Here, the space is navy and white, a classic seaside scheme. To soften the boundary between inside and out, she installed French doors that open onto the swimming pool, whirlpool and shade cabana with chaises she introduced outside to replace a small backyard. Topped by a transom and flanked with sidelights, the doors let in plenty of daylight. The high ceiling is covered with white-painted planks and beams that give the room a cottagey quality that has been opened up to the rafters.

COOL AND CONTEMPORARY

Set amid a deep lot located in Bethesda, Maryland, planted with trees, a modern cube of a house built in the early 1960s had hidden potential that owners Elliott Himmelfarb and Janet Minker fully exploited by gradually remodeling it over several years. After turning their yard into an English-style garden, they enlisted architects Lee Quill and Ralph Cunningham of Cunngham & Quill to give the boxy house new energy with an addition that would turn its plan into an L-shape. Perched atop the new 900-square-foot addition like a tree house is a new master suite with windows, some floor-to-ceiling, on all four sides, affording the couple soothing views of their garden. The windows, including a slender horizontal band that Janet and Elliott call the "mail slot," also allow natural light to pour into the inviting space. "At night we can track the moon through the clerestory windows," says Elliott. "In the morning we can see the birds come and go at the bird feeder."

above In the master bedroom addition, it's navy and white, a seaside classic. Seagrass matting and grasscloth wallpaper add island-flavored texture. The plank ceiling gives the feel of a cottage that's been opened up to the rafters.

Like the rest of the house, the suite is furnished sparely, and an adjacent new bathroom features unobtrusive luxuries like a skylight over the shower and radiant heat under the limestone floor, which cycles up and down on a thermostat.

right A drawing by artist Jody Mussoff injects a note of contrasting color on a bedside table. below The view into the wooded lot is the bedroom's main attraction. Roller blinds tucked above the windows can be lowered for complete privacy and darkness. A Le Corbusier chaise offers an extra place to lounge near the window. The cast-aluminum Skeleton chair is by Michael Aram. The colors in the new master suite are soothing and spalike. far right Pocket doors to the bedroom, bathroom and walk-in closet help keep the addition uncluttered. The corridor and bedroom flooring is sustainable bamboo.

Creating a Comfortable, Clutter-Free Sanctuary

After adding a wing to a 1940s Arts and Crafts–style house in surburban Washington, DC, architect Charles Moore expanded the second story to gain more square footage for private spaces, including the master bedroom. An array of hues—from quiet neutrals to a lively robin's-egg blue—were used to define rooms on the lower level. In the upstairs master bedroom, the wall tone shifts to soft sage- green. "It works well with brown, green or blue linens," says owner Andrea Roberson of the versatile hue.

With windows on three sides, the master bedroom gets sun all day, so the architect added simple white wooden shutters to control the light. This cozy retreat is the only place in the house where Andrea and her husband, Scott, used wall-to-wall carpeting. Moore designed the bedroom like a hotel suite, with space for only a bed, side tables and lamps. "There's no place to stack stuff," says Andrea, whose dressers and hanging clothes are stored neatly in an adjacent walk-in closet. "When you have a big family, stacks can start to pile up," says Andrea, who conscientiously finds a place for everything. "The trick is being able to close doors."

With windows on three sides, the master bedroom gets sun all day. Simple white wooden shutters can control the light. This room is the only place in the house where the owners installed wall-to-wall carpeting.

Closet Organizing Ideas from the Pros

The average person cleans out their closet only every two to five years, according to Toronto-based designer Glen Peloso, a certified professional organizer and host of the Canadian television program *Renovate My Wardrobe.* To find out how to stay a step ahead of a jammed-up closet, consider this advice from both Peloso and Shannon McGinnis, another certified professional organizer:

- **TAKE ON THE TASK IN BABY STEPS.** Doing so keeps it from feeling so daunting, says McGinnis. When you're ready to purge and reorder your closet, she suggests setting a timer for 10 minutes, then going through as much as you can in that time. Begin on one end of your closet and pull out items that can be given away, folded instead of hung or stored elsewhere for the season. Depending on your progress, when the time is up, you can either reset for another 10 minutes and keep going, or start again later. You'll likely need a few rounds to finish.

- **EDIT AND REGROUP.** Once you've weeded out extraneous clothing, take a look at what's left and think about how best to organize it. Investing in a system like the one pictured here will help you maximize storage. "One of the biggest problems people have is that they are looking at the floor space when really the wall space is the most valuable area," says Peloso. He recommends thinking vertically. Creating two short hanging spaces instead of one long one, for example, can actually double your hanging space. Remember, you can fit more into an organized closet than a cluttered one!

- **DIVIDE YOUR CLOSET INTO ZONES.** One area should be dedicated to items used every day, one to those used occasionally, and the last to those used infrequently. Your everyday items should be most accessible—between waist and eye level.

- **SHELVE IT.** Reserve high shelves for infrequently used items, like special-occasion accessories or cold-weather layers. The highest shelf should be no more than 6 feet 3 inches from the floor or the average person will need a stepladder to reach it.

- **KEEP VALUABLES HIDDEN.** Drawers are great for storing small items or jewelry. If you're storing disparate items in a drawer, use organizers to keep the bottom of the drawer from becoming the "ignore pile," says Peloso. Stow jewelry and accessories in boxes or inside cabinet doors, where they'll be safe from dust and out of children's reach. A shallow tray can corral small frequently used items, such as watches, everyday earrings or sunglasses.

- **REIN IN STACKS.** Folded clothing can get messy quickly, so keep casual pieces in baskets or bins that you can pull off the shelf, or stow them in stackable boxes, which allow you to make better use of vertical space. Wire slide-out drawers keep purses visible and easy to grab. If you like to match your purse with your belt, store perfect pairs together.

- **MAKE USE OF SPACE DOWN UNDER.** You're more likely to wear all of your shoes if you can see them and don't have to search for pairs. Store them in clear shoe drawers at the bottom of your closet or place them side by side on shoe racks, which can be stacked to hold multiple pairs of shoes.

- **HANG IT UP.** Don't fill your closet with wire hangers from the dry cleaner's—the thin metal can leave wrinkle marks or rust stains. "The average woman needs a few different kinds of hangers or a multifunction hanger," says Peloso. A wooden or foam hanger with indented shoulder sections and a cross bar with clips will accommodate suits, shirts, pants and skirts.

Using Tubular Hangers in your favorite color might be incentive enough to keep your closet organized. In Bubblegum Pink, The Container Store.

Padded Zebra Hangers keep blouse and jacket shoulders wrinkle-free. Creative Containers.

The extra-skinny Ultra Slim Hangers are flocked to prevent straps from slipping. In Camel, Bed Bath & Beyond.

Soft-Touch Skirt & Trouser Clamp Hangers keep skirt tops from stretching with a flat clamp instead of clips. In Pink, The Container Store.

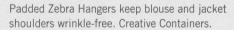

All About Flooring

Money-Wise Floor Tips: Renew, Repair or Replace

Flooring is one of the costliest elements in a home—and one of the most important contributors to its value. If you have dull or damaged wood floors, you have four ways to improve them:

- Clean and polish
- Abrade and recoat with a new finish
- Sand, stain and refinish
- Replace with new floors

To determine which option is best for you, a superior floor care resource is the Swedish company Bona. It offers a full range of maintenance solutions from its Greenguard certified Hardwood Floor Care System to its dust-free sanding system, and provides DIY and professional refinishing options.

Cleaning and polishing 500 square feet of wood flooring with a Bona kit costs about $40, while abrading and recoating might cost between $3 and $6 per square foot, and replacing the flooring could cost from $6 to $12 or more per square foot, including installation, depending on the type of wood floor you choose, the conditions of your subfloor and whether or not the flooring is prefinished. For more information, visit *bona.com*.

MATERIAL	PROS	CONS	COST
BAMBOO AND CORK	■ Durable ■ From renewable resources ■ Comes prefinished ■ Warm, natural look	■ Limited palette of colors and patterns ■ Cork requires some maintenance	■ Bamboo, $5.50 to $8.50 per square foot; cork, $7 to $13 per square foot
CARPET	■ Soft underfoot ■ Available in natural or synthetic fibers ■ Many colors and patterns	■ Can become matted in high-traffic areas ■ May stain ■ Can harbor mold, dust and pet dander	■ $18 and up per square yard (carpet and pad)
CERAMIC TILE AND STONE	■ Extremely durable ■ Wide range of colors and patterns ■ Very low maintenance ■ Resists water damage	■ Cold underfoot in winter ■ Grout may stain ■ Can be slippery when wet	■ Tile, $2.75 to $20 per square foot; $7 and up for natural stone
ENGINEERED WOOD	■ More stable than solid wood in high-moisture environments ■ Available in variety of colors and species ■ Often sold prefinished	■ Surface can be dented and scratched ■ Thin top layer limits the number of times it can be refinished	■ $5.25 to $17.50 per square foot
LAMINATE	■ Durable-wear layer ■ Available as tiles or planks ■ Can be installed over existing floor	■ Can't be refinished ■ Can show swelling if core becomes damp ■ Thin planks may sound tinny underfoot	■ $2 to $10.50 per square foot
LINOLEUM	■ Resilient and durable ■ Made with natural ingredients ■ Many colors and patterns ■ Available in sheets or tiles	■ More expensive than vinyl ■ Sheet flooring should be installed by professional ■ Needs occasional polish	■ $7 to $10 per square foot
SOLID WOOD	■ Natural warmth and beauty ■ Available in many species and grain patterns ■ Can be refinished a number of times	■ Shrinks and expands with changes in moisture content ■ Surface can dent or scratch	■ $5.50 to $22 per square foot
VINYL	■ Resilient surface ■ Not affected by water ■ Available in many patterns and colors ■ Low-maintenance	■ Seams between sheets may be visible or lift ■ Patterns may wear or fade	■ $1.25 to $7 per square foot

Caring for Floors to Enhance Home Value

In today's economic climate, where uncertainty rules, there's nothing more important than protecting the value of your most prized material possession—your home.

The World Floor Covering Association (WFCA), the country's leading advocacy organization for the flooring trade. has conducted research on flooring that can help consumers make smart investments in their home with the goal of increasing and maintaining value. Certain aspects of a house can increase its value, its curb appeal and subsequently, its sale. And one of the most important features of a home is its flooring. Why? Because flooring is typically one of the single most expensive investments a consumer will ever make. It beats roofs, windows and sometimes even room additions.

Maintaining and increasing the value of your home does not necessarily mean replacing your floors. Flooring can be one of the most valuable commodities in a house and also one of the least expensive to maintain and improve. A few simple techniques offered by the WFCA that cost virtually nothing but your time may help extend the life of your flooring:

- For natural flooring products such as wood, never use ammonia cleaners or oil soaps. They will dull the finish and performance of your floor. These products will also affect the ability to recoat your floor later on down the road.
- Since wood naturally expands when it's wet, never wet mop or use excessive water to clean your hardwood floor. Large amounts of water can cause the wood to swell and may cause your planks or strips to crack or splinter. Be sure to wipe up spills on your hardwood promptly.
- Pets with long nails can cause dents and scratches on hardwood floors that are not covered by your warranty. Be sure to regularly trim your pet's claws to avoid damage.
- You may not realize it, but carpet is the largest filter in a home or building. It filters soils, gases, allergens, spills and other pollutants. With this in mind, it is important to vacuum regularly and to use a manufacturer-approved cleaning product.
- To avoid running into warranty issues with your carpet (and many other types of flooring), make sure you use cleaning products recommended by the floor's manufacturer. Using some cleaners and certain chemicals on your floors can void its warranty. The Carpet and Rug Institute Seal of Approval program identifies effective carpet cleaning solutions and equipment, and these products fall within the guidelines of carpet manufacturer warranty programs.
- Protect the finish on laminate, hardwood, carpet or resilient floors from the harmful rays of direct sunlight by using window shades and closing drapes. It's also a good idea to periodically rotate rugs and furniture exposed to direct sunlight so your floors don't develop unwanted "tan lines" and discoloration.
- Try to clean up spills as quickly as possible on ceramic floors so that the grout or tile doesn't become stained. Don't use bleach or ammonia-based cleaners, as these products can discolor your grout if used too often. And don't clean glazed tile with oil-based cleaners. While ceramic tile is considered very durable, it's not indestructible and may crack or chip under extreme force.
- With ceramic floors, after the installation process is complete and the grout has had ample time to cure, sealing the grout and tile can provide protection from dirt and spills by slowing down the staining process. It's your responsibility to seal your floors—not the installer's—unless you request it.
- With vinyl floors, avoid using rubber-backed mats or rugs, as they can damage and potentially discolor your floor. Instead, use mats or rugs made especially for vinyl floors and remember to treat them accordingly.
- With all stone floors, always blot spills immediately. A neutral pH detergent or pure soap, such as Ivory Liquid and warm water, can be used for spills or periodic cleaning. Don't use products that contain lemon juice, vinegar or other acids on marble, limestone or travertine. You should avoid using products that contain abrasive cleaners, cleansers (dry or soft) or any ammonia-based cleaners on any stone. These products will dull stone's luster. Also, don't use scouring powders or bathroom tub-and-tile cleaners on your stone.

Case Studies

Case Study 1: Nursery Room Makeover

Soon-to-be-parents Kathleen and Jared Reitzin envisioned a wonderful room for their first child. Like most young couples today, though, they wanted to create a nursery without depleting their savings. Not a huge fan of fussy pink themes, Kathleen was imagining a sophisticated palette of light pink and chocolate brown to better fit the hip tone of their Encino-area, California, townhouse. The existing room, she recalls, "was all blah and boring. I wanted it to be baby-appropriate but a little more adult. And I love the color chocolate. We also hoped to somehow include our daughter's name—Kayla Kai."

To help them create the ideal nursery, the couple enlisted designer Erinn Valencich, who is owner of Omniarte Design in Los Angeles and has fashioned kids' rooms for clients around the country. To ensure the Reitzins got the nursery of their dreams, Valencich devised a savvy, cost-effective plan that kicked off with a burst of color. Here's her recipe for the perfect baby room.

INJECT FRESHNESS WITH PAINT AND PERSONALITY. The first move was painting the walls: chocolate next to the dressing table, jaunty stripes flanking the sitting area and light pink beside the crib. Then, to boost the charm factor, Valencich painted eight squares of darker pink on the lightest wall to showcase wooden craft-store letters spelling out the baby's name. Satin ribbons glued and stapled to the back of each letter are nailed to the top of the wall. "Erinn told us getting creative with paint would change everything. The results were phenomenal," says Kathleen.

ADD FLEXIBLE FURNISHINGS. An heirloom cradle (made by Jared's grandfather) and a handsome crib were already in place. But Mom still needed a rocker for nursing, a changing table and storage. Rather than spend money on juvenile pieces, Kathleen and Jared looked to ModernNursery.com for affordable items that would grow along with their daughter: a modern-style lacquer cabinet (with removable changing pad) for stashing diapers and onesies, a complementary nightstand with two drawers to handle the overflow and a cool rocker with a high back for support.

WELCOME BOLD COLORS. For curtains, Erinn found a print with a grownup twist—in the perfect color family—and cleverly combined it with solid-colored linen. "Mixing a little bit of expensive fabric with less costly cloth is a great way to stretch a budget," she says. A vibrant pink Meridian area rug perks up the plain-vanilla carpet.

bottom Kayla Kai's personalized sleeping area is the focal point. A beguiling 100-percent-wool carpet makes the setting cozy. Stuffed toys climb aboard the outgrown cradle. **below** Before Erinn redesigned the nursery, the room felt dreary and lacked sufficient storage.

ADD MEANINGFUL—NOT COSTLY—ACCESSORIES. Talk about bang for your buck: A parade of favorite photos enlarged on the computer and popped into ready-made frames provides a happy show for baby and all the family to enjoy for a long time to come.

Kid-Friendly Style

Make it safe, long-term and easy-care. Here's how:

- **FLEXIBLE FURNITURE** that grows with your child—like a crib that converts to a toddler's bed—is an investment for the future. Use low- or zero-VOC paint to eliminate harmful vapors.
- **HARDWOOD FLOORS,** all-natural fiber rugs and quality bedding also help provide a healthier environment.
- **OPT FOR COTTON OR LINEN** curtains and shades (secure cords safely out of reach) to regulate sun at nap time.
- **INTRODUCE A COMBINATION** of open and closed storage (check out Kayla Kai's trio of penny-saving repurposed boxes, above) to organize supplies, clothes and toys.
- **ALWAYS SELECT BABY-APPROVED PRODUCTS** for cleaning everything from changing tables to teddy bears.

above left For extra punch, hot pink grosgrain ribbon offsets the geometric Osborne & Little fabric. Teamed with light-diffusing sheers, the window treatment is striking and functional. **above center** Years from now, Kayla Kai will find lots of reasons to love her contemporary nightstand. Kathleen uses the pretty gift boxes—recycled from her baby shower—to hold tiny essentials like swabs and cotton balls. **above** Graphic random-width stripes lend visual interest to a quiet corner, as does a bright accent pillow. Water- and stain-resistant, the Ultrasuede rocker with matching stool is durable and chic enough to please a teen someday. **left** Valencich painted wooden letters a rich brown before affixing them to the wall. A cloth sleeve gives the whimsical crib mobile a custom look. **below** Toys in coordinating colors are decorative touches, too. These soft alphabet blocks, turned any which way, are a perfect example.

Case Study 2: Small Space Makeover

Designer Libby Langdon, who often appeared as an expert on HGTV's *Small Space, Big Style,* was asked to transform this small master bedroom into an inviting retreat. It was undistinguished, with no architectural details to draw on for design inspiration. Its white walls were bland, and unrelated bursts of color on window shades and in artwork made the space feel chaotic. Furnishings were a hodgepodge of leftovers, giving the space a cluttered feeling. The room has two windows and a sliding door overlooking a pool and spacious yard, but still felt closed-in and dark.

Here's how Langdon gave her client a cozy bedroom that combines the spirit of a peaceful spa and a chic hotel.

KEEP IT COOL. Since the home is used mostly in warmer months, Langdon selected a cooling summery palette of pale blue and warm tans. The peaceful colors also unify and expand the space and let the eye gravitate toward the outdoor views. "Too many colors can make a space feel chopped up and even smaller," Langdon says.

LET IN AND CONTROL LIGHT. Before the makeover, bright yellow shades overpowered the windows. "If you're going to have a bold, colorful window treatment, you need a substantial wall color to balance the impact," Langdon says. Instead, she installed sheer panels high on the wall, which soften edges without cutting into the light. "In a small space, hang the rod at or near the ceiling," she says. "It draws the eye up and makes the ceiling appear higher and the room larger." She also added window shades for privacy.

CLEAR OUT AND SCALE UP. The key in a small space is to go big but avoid clutter. "A small room will appear even smaller if you fill it with little things," Langdon says. A large headboard, upholstered in linen, brings height and weight to the once-bland wall; tall lamps—29 to 32 inches high—balance the scale of the headboard. Replacing the fussy rattan chairs and table with a sleek but cushy chair and ottoman creates a reading corner. And instead of the old rug, which looked like

below Placed to reflect sunlight, the oversize mirror visually doubles the room's size; its dark frame adds a sense of weight to the light colors that define the room. Small touches, such as the tufting on the headboard and beige trim around edges of bed linens, give the streamlined room some eye-catching details.

a postage stamp on the floor, a new Berber rug adds softness, while its large size expands the room.

USE CLEVER STORAGE ELEMENTS. Three-drawer chests use a little more floor space, but Langdon prefers them to nightstands. "You gain a lot of storage with them," she says, "and they make the space feel luxurious." For storing bed linens, she added a double-duty linen-covered bench/chest at the foot of the bed.

EMPLOY SPACE-EXPANDING TRICKS. "If you can position a mirror opposite a window," Langdon says, "it will reflect natural light and visually double the size of a room." Here, she opted for a large mirror propped against the wall. "It gives the room the feel of a hip, chic boutique hotel."

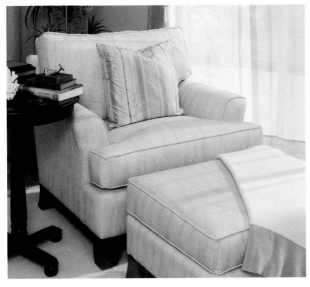

above Hanging sheer draperies in line with the ceiling break adds to the sense of height and makes the windows appear larger, while artwork echoes the room's soothing colors. **left** Langdon placed a comfortable chair for reading in a corner near the window to take advantage of sunlight and the view of the pool. A plant adds height and interest to the corner.

Space-Stretching Tips

- **GO BOLD WITH COLOR.** Color is the least expensive way to make a statement. Try bold color on an accent wall. Or use cool tones, such as sky-blue or aqua, which appear to recede and make a room look larger.

- **ADD PUNCH WITH ARTWORK.** Even in a small space, an empty wall will look cold. Posters are inexpensive, and there's such a variety. Create a display of pictures with a similar theme: A grid of smaller prints has the effect of one large piece. Frame a series of botanicals taken from old books, or make black-and-white blowups of family photos. Simple frames, big mats, you're set!

- **KEEP THINGS LIGHT.** If a small space is dark, it's going to look even smaller. Bring in some light. Large lamps add height and scale to a small space. You can also give lamps you already have a facelift with paint, a taller harp and a new shade. Try covering the shade with fabric to match your decor.

- **REFLECT ON YOUR SURROUNDINGS.** Mirrors—the bigger the better—are a great way to expand a room visually. Placing a mirror opposite a window will reflect the light and the view. Shop for interesting mirrors in thrift shops and home-improvement stores. Or create an eye-catching wall arrangement of beveled mirror tiles.

- **BRING IN TEXTURED FABRICS.** Silk, microsuede, linen and bouclé are all great fabrics that add texture and warmth without bringing in busy patterns, which can be distracting in a small space. Big patterns can also overwhelm, but if there's one you absolutely love, use it in small accents. Shop the sales and outlet stores for good buys, and choose a solid neutral for big pieces like draperies or headboards. Hang draperies high—drawing the eye up will make a space feel larger.

- **MIX AND MATCH.** Furniture sets often have more items than you need and can overwhelm a small room. It's more interesting to combine different pieces that you've gathered and make the space your own. Be sure to include some double-duty storage pieces.

Case Study 3: Creating a Grown-Up Teen's Room

A teenager's room should be a sanctuary, a special haven—a spot in which to hang out and do the things you like best. For Kate Wasserbach, a 16-year-old with grownup, urbane taste and plans for a career in fashion, sewing is her thing, and she needed a place to do it.

Kate's bedroom was spacious, like the rest of her family's circa-1940 home in Loudenville, New York. But time had taken its toll. A rising tide of books and teenage clutter was gaining ground in every corner. Even the cute window seat where Kate liked to read had lost its appeal.

Ruling out a disruptive renovation, Kate's family enlisted her aunt, decorator Joanne Hans, for a total makeover. The goal: a haven where Kate could feel creatively inspired. That, and put her things away.

Aunt Joanne's starting point was to pick a theme, and

top Warm wood, toile-patterned wallpaper, and cheery pink and graphic faux-zebra accents make this freshly redecorated room almost grown up, but still fun. above A room in need of a serious style update. below Beneath a ceiling fan that had to go, a gallery of personal photos climbed the walls, while a beige carpet lent no cheer.

a color scheme. Rather than the little girls' perennial favorite purple-and-pink combination that Joanne had envisioned, Kate surprised her. Her requests? Black and white. And, toile de Jouy—the traditional 18th-century fabric, block-printed with bucolic scenes. So black-and-white toile it would be.

"Kate and I went to a local wallpaper store and asked them for every available book with toile," Joanne laughs. Joanne suggested that her 21st-century niece paper just two walls, then paint the rest a clean, serene white. "Too much pattern can be overwhelming," she explained. Then she revved up the sophistication by glazing the existing bifold closet doors, built-in bureaus that flank the bed, and window seat—all in striking semigloss black.

Next, Kate's hand-me-down furniture, dated fabrics and beige carpet were shown the door. Instead, Joanne specified the handsome four-poster, dresser, mirror and night tables that now enliven the room and provide the aspiring fashion designer with all the storage a girl could need. A splurge, even with her to-the-trade discounts, Joanne knew that the new furnishings would be heirlooms Kate could keep for many years to come. A faux-zebra rug and matching chair fabric riff on the black-and-white theme.

Joanne also angled in a work surface for sewing and drawing, supported on components that provide cubbies to boost the room's storage. A cabinet keeps files and swatches orderly, and a wall-mounted calendar provides more nooks for supplies.

These days, when Kate feels like lounging, she can sprawl on her bed beneath a dainty chandelier that took the place of an old ceiling fan. Or she can hold court on her freshly upholstered window seat, all polka-dots and crisp black welting. Perched on a nest of adorable cushions, she's as cozy and content as can be.

What Was Done

- **WALLPAPERED** two walls with Kate's favorite toile pattern, and painted the other two.
- **PAINTED** the original built-ins, closet doors and window seat semigloss black.
- **REPLACED** the carpet and added a graphic faux-zebra rug.
- **RETAINED** the original layout, and substituted new, grown-up furnishings for old.
- **SWAPPED** the ceiling fan for a sweet chandelier.
- **COMMISSIONED** a window shade, and ordered a monogram to personalize it.
- **PURCHASED** new bed linens and accessories.

above left Framed by a pair of inexpensive glass lamps, a mirror visually expands the room. The bureau doubles as a dressing table. **above right** A charming window seat was constructed beneath an eave (in background). Anchoring one corner of the room, a custom work surface sits on readymade cubbies that neatly house supplies and accessories. **right** Wallpaper and black paint emphasize drawers, built into the eaves, a charming feature original to the house that proved well worth preserving. **below** Kate's original work space was drab and forlorn.

BEFORE

CREATING CURB APPEAL AND INVITING OUTDOOR SPACES

WHETHER IT'S IN THE CITY OR IN THE COUNTRY, large or small, the facade of your home leaves a first and lasting impression, as does the landscape that surrounds it. Picture the possibilities: a charming paved path, perhaps, leading past neat beds of flowers to a stately entrance, or a walkway of rough-hewn stones, winding through pockets of plush, green shrubs toward an arbor-topped gate covered with a canopy of swirling vines. Simple, creative outdoor touches like these will not only uplift the spirits of family and friends, they'll enhance your home's curb appeal—and elevate its value.

Simple DIY spruce-ups like introducing containers filled with flowering plants or adorning the front door with a wreath add color, energy and life in practically no time, and at very low cost. A new deck, patio or garden structure will naturally require more time and money, but with the right planning and materials, still don't have to break the bank. Whether you apply your own sweat equity or enlist the help of pros, any investment you make in enhancing the front of your home will be worth many happy returns.

This charming shingled shed with its shaded seat is both a focal point and destination, drawing the visitor down the path and providing a comfy spot for looking out and viewing the garden. It also offers a retreat from the sun or a sudden downpour while working in the garden. The soft, blue-gray color of the shingles captures the hues of the lavender plants in full bloom. The architecture is classic and is complemented by the picket fence beyond that further encloses the space. The arched doorway echoes the shape of the metal armillary sphere. The hip-roofed, wood-shingled shed can be designed, built and installed by a carpenter, or a similar structure can be found at places that sell premade sheds ready for delivery to your site.

Gates, Gardens, Hardscape Elements and Paths

Gates and Gardens

To create an inviting entrance that will let your guests know that you welcome their visit, choose decorative elements that complement the style and architecture of your home—they'll go a long way toward achieving that goal. A safe, sturdy walkway, proper lighting, a welcome mat and a doorbell to announce the arrival of visitors are necessary utilities. Topping off these essentials with living plants sporting interesting foliage and colorful blooms will give your entranceway an extra edge. Not only will these elements enrich the curb appeal of your home, they'll also provide hints of what your guests can expect to see when they enter. Constructed extras like a gate topped with an arbor will add both function and character. Understated gates can be made special affordably by adding interesting hardware or embellishing them with a whimsical door knocker.

Simple fixes like hanging baskets filled with trailing plants, plants in containers grouped near the steps, a wreath on the door or an interesting mailbox can also be added to any home to boost the beauty quotient for a low cost. Container gardens are the perfect way to add splashes of color to your yard, deck, porch or patio. Whether planted with your favorite flowers, trailing vines, tasty herbs and veggies, or tightly clipped small-scale shrubs, they are potted pleasures that are fun and easy to create.

The trick to successful container gardens is to choose pots and plants that coordinate with the style of your home and your personal taste. Select classic vessels like urns or adorned boxes planted with tiny shrubs for a traditional look. Choose sleek, modern shapes filled with spiky-leaved plants for contemporary settings. Or consider filling a weathered wheelbarrow or watering can with old-fashioned flowers to enliven a country setting.

Placement is also key. Set your container garden at the end of walkway as a welcoming note, or hang a basket filled with colorful plants from a porch post as a vibrant focal point. You can also define an entrance with a pair of matching containers or place a fragrant plant on a deck. Whatever your gardening skill level, a planted pot is a simple way to enrich your outdoor environs and show a little personality, too. Where you can, change the potted plants and accents such as doormats and cushions on your porch seating with the seasons. Your guests will feel welcome any time of the year.

below This classic foursquare, with its wide porch, has out-of-the-box panache and great curb appeal. The absence of extravagant architectural detail allows shape to define the style of the home. Typifying the vernacular is its precise symmetry. The vertical midline flows visually from front door to second-level window to the home's crown jewel—a shuttered dormer. The hip roof with overhang and lap siding widen the profile and equalize the square. Earthy autumn hues, borrowed from the Arts and Crafts era, colored the foursquares of the 1890s to 1930s. Here, burnt-red siding, an understated slate-gray door and wheat-toned columns and trim make a confident color statement. Double-hung windows are framed by shutters and topped with a decorative cornice. The effect is neat and orderly. The symmetrical style is echoed on the expansive front porch, with its pair of hanging baskets and twin lanterns. Rockers and a well-displayed flag complete the look.

above When a pathway is desired but the budget is tight, using recycled materials is a great money-saver. This do-it-yourself garden walk, perfect for a stroll from the street to the front door, was made of salvaged slates, all in similar natural tones for uniformity. The key is to level the surface and fill the space with clean sand before installing the paving materials. The tall double gate topped with an arbor and adorned with wreathes practically shouts hello!

above This covered gate acts as a portal to the front yard and provides a welcoming exterior doorway to the path and garden leading to the front door of the house. The design of the gate echoes the mullioned glass door and windows of the house. The overhead arbor further echoes the portico over the front door. The gateway is inserted into the shrubbery for a secret-garden feel and helps establish the cottage-style look of the garden and house. It's best to have a gate like this installed by a carpenter to ensure that it operates properly. **far left** Add a splash of color to a predominately green garden bed with an old washtub filled with cheerful purple pansies. For a major color infusion, hang a basket of petunias in a similar hue from a nearby tree branch. Be sure to punch some holes in the bottom of the galvanized metal tub for drainage. **left** The coping of a pool is the perfect spot to place colorful container gardens. They can be moved out of the way at the end of the season when it's time to cover the pool for the winter. These cobalt-blue glazed pots in varying sizes echo the cool blue liner of the pool and their square shapes help enhance the straight architectural lines of the paving stones they sit on. Filled with Bloodleaf, coleus, grasses and cannas, all in similar colors, the arrangement lends a tropical touch to this sunny spot—perfect for the poolside.

Seasonal Updates

You might not change the solid elements of your home like pathways, porches, doors and railings every few months, but you can change the plants and accessories you use to decorate your house seasonally. Trees and shrubs remain in place, but container plants, cushions and doormats can be updated to go with the seasons of the year. Here are some suggestions.

- **GET READY FOR SPRING** by filling containers with pots of already blooming violas, tulips or daffodils. Simply remove the soil from your containers and pop in a pot of blooming spring plants, which are grown in greenhouses and readily available at most garden centers in early spring. While you are shopping for plants, grab a new doormat in a pretty spring pattern or color to replace the worn-out one that's been working hard all winter.

- **WHEN SUMMER ARRIVES,** replace the fading spring flowers in your containers with summer annuals that will bloom all season long. Choose plants in hues that will complement the colors of your house. For traditional-style homes, try the updated classics like the new varieties of geraniums, new colors of impatiens and the host of tender perennials that are widely available at garden centers. For contemporary-style homes, choose architectural plants like agave, phormiums, and bamboo, each planted in its own modern container. Summer is also a good time to update cushions of porch furniture with new colors and patterns.

- **AS THE WEATHER COOLS,** pull out spent summer plants and toss in the compost. Replace them with tiny evergreens like Alberta spruce, boxwoods or small junipers that will stay green all winter long. Garden centers carry plants at this time of year specifically for the cold-weather season. For the holidays, string tiny white lights among their branches and add pumpkins, gourds and ornamental cabbage plants for the fall. Switch out your summer porch cushions for autumnal colored pillows and toss a warm throw on a chair for a cozy look. Replace your doormat with one that will be sure to scrape off winter snow and mud.

Container Garden Tips

Potted gardens are easy to make, but you should take care to meet their needs so they grow healthy and full all season long. Follow these tips for best results.

- **MAKE SURE ALL THE PLANTS** you put in one pot require the same sun and water. Don't mix shade lovers with sun worshipers.

- **AT THE NURSERY,** choose the plants and arrange them as you would plant them in the pot to be sure they look good together. Mix textures of both flowers and foliage for a natural look.

- **IN LARGER CONTAINERS,** place a sheet of landscape fabric in the bottom of the pot, fill about halfway with Styrofoam packing peanuts, add another sheet of the fabric, then fill with good potting soil. This will help keep the pot light enough to move.

- **USE A LIGHTWEIGHT POTTING SOIL** specifically designed for containers. Do not use garden soil, as it will compact down over time and the plants will suffer. Buy a soil mix already fortified with nutrients the plants will need to flower.

- **CONTAINER GARDENS DRY OUT QUICKLY** in midsummer and may need watering more than once a day. Installing a drip irrigation system will help keep plants properly watered. Make sure all of your containers have holes in the bottom for good drainage.

- **REMOVE SPENT FLOWERS** often so new shoots will come up and flower again. This will help extend the beauty of your containers throughout the growing season.

Tech Tip: Smart Sprinkler

Wouldn't it be great if your sprinkler system could respond to the weather? The Cyber-Rain Sprinkler Controller system does just that, adjusting the amount of watering you need with Internet-based weather forecasts linked to your zip code. Cyber-Rain handles up to eight zones, each one independently controlled. You can manage the duration and number of waterings per day, name and tag the zones with photos from your yard, and put zones on hold when necessary. Customized features include soak and fertilizer settings. $399. 877-888-1452; *cyber-rain.com*

Sometimes nature tells us exactly where to put a resting spot in our yards. These stone steps and the adjoining built-in bench fit perfectly into the rocky shoreline of this waterside setting. The bench is the ideal spot for taking in the soothing view of the water while offering a place to pause before ascending the steps to the rise in the yard. Moving boulders of this size is tough work and requires heavy-duty machinery to position the stones safely and properly, so it's a job best left to the professionals. However, a similar effect can be achieved by carving out a spot in a hillside and placing a sturdy wooden bench or even a seating wall made of mortared-in-place stone.

Hardscape Elements

Autumn's arrival doesn't mean the whole garden has to head to sleep for half the year. As the perennials send out their last blooms, hardscape elements—such as sheds, benches, pergolas and gates—that make up the "bones" of a garden become more apparent, so the landscape just takes on another dimension. As leaves drop off and blossoms fade, these structures will stand out even more as focal points, destinations and guideposts along your walkways.

In Victorian times, elaborately designed structures signified wealth and status, but on the practical side, they offered storage, a retreat from the hot sun or a sudden downpour, or defined the boundaries of the property. In today's gardens, these structures continue to offer practical solutions. Who doesn't need more space to store the bicycles, lawnmower or garden tools? A gazebo is a great place to entertain away from the house, a sort of local retreat that might offer another view of the yard. A fence and gate topped by an arbor gives climbing vines a place to thrive and can keep the dog from straying too far.

The key to using these structures successfully—whether you build them yourself or buy prefabricated versions—is to make sure they complement the architecture of your house. Cute, cottage-style sheds look great with classic shingle-style homes, as do traditional white-painted gazebos and arbors. A streamlined pergola or a simply framed shed would blend nicely with a contemporary home.

To express your personality and taste, use paint or other decorative touches. A prefab shed, for example, takes on a playful air if the trim is brightly colored. It will also stand out against the gray winter days ahead. A gaily painted oversize birdhouse will add a pop of color long after the blooms have faded. The birds don't really care what color their house is! Whatever structure you choose to add to your garden, it will be a permanent reminder when you look out your window on a cold winter's day that spring is sure to come again.

Get Inspired

There is no better way to discover the beauty and practicality of garden structures than to visit public and private gardens that have them. You can also reference books, magazines and websites that feature gardens that use structures in their layouts. Consider these additional ideas for inspiration:

- **VISIT PRIVATE GARDENS** in your area located through the Open Days Directory, an annual publication that lists, by state and region, private gardens that are open for visiting on specific days from the spring through fall for a nominal fee. The guide also offers tips on the best times to visit public gardens. Visit *gardenconservancy.org*.

- **PLAN A TRIP TO HISTORICAL SITES** such as Colonial Williamsburg, the gardens at Versailles, or nearly any botanical garden in your area. They are chockful of gates, sheds and garden structures that will inspire your design decisions.

- **NOTE THE WAYS** in which garden structures are used in public spaces, such as local parks or plazas. A town center, for example, might have a gazebo, which will show you how the structure was made and where it is placed to take advantage of a pretty view.

- **CONSULT WITH A GARDEN DESIGNER** or landscape architect. They are experts at placing garden structures on your property to maximize views and create a flow around your yard.

left An oversize birdfeeder designed in a classic style complements the traditional design of the lattice fence and arbor bordering this garden. Set on a stout post, it is easy to access for adding seed or cleaning. The small size of the roofing shingles, siding and windows keeps the whole structure in scale. Climbing vines, wispy ornamental grasses and flecks of colorful perennials offer typical textures to cottage-style gardens. Similar feeders can be purchased via the Internet or easily built in any style by a handy homeowner.

above Even a simple tuteur set in a garden bed draws the eye up from the colorful blooms surrounding it. It gives climbing vegetable plants, such as beans and peas, something to cling to and allows the flowerbed to do double duty. It is easily purchased online or at a garden center; just put it in place and let the magic happen. It will instantly transform a single-level plot into a multitasking terrain.

Paths

There's nothing like a stroll through nature to take the edge off a long, hard day. But you don't have to head for the hills to take a refreshing hike. A sturdy, well-defined path gives visitors to your home a strong first impression. It must be wide enough to accommodate two people walking side by side. It should also be clean and hint at the style of your house, giving guests a glimpse of what they can expect to see inside. Crafting a simple garden path is relatively easy to do in your own backyard, though creating more sophisticated pathways does require professional help. The trick is to select one that suits the site. Whether you want a moment to meditate or to take a little time to smell the roses, there's a garden path that's right for you and your yard.

Creating privacy in a shallow backyard can be achieved by fooling the eye. This professionally installed pathway, made of cut and mortared slates, skirts the back of the house and provides a destination for enjoying the yard. The pergola draws the eye up to the open sky and complements the updated traditional architecture of the home. A pocket patio for the bench acts as a focal point when looking out the window to the yard—and a place to sit and admire the garden bed under the window. The straight lines of the stones point to an open gate at the edge of the lawn, leading the eye beyond the yard.

Formal settings need not be straight-laced. In fact, it makes for a more interesting journey through a yard if a garden pathway meanders a bit, allowing the plantings to reveal themselves along the way. This professionally installed granite-block path is bordered by clipped boxwood bushes that define the edges, help contain the lush flowering plants and allow just a bit of their beauty to spill out and soften the edges of the path. Between the pavers, low-growing plants that can withstand the crush of footfalls tie the garden to the path. Unobtrusive light fixtures in patinated metal illuminate the way.

Turning a steep slope into usable outdoor space can be a challenge. Installing wide grass steps with stone block risers not only does the trick, it also makes a grand statement. Doing this project yourself may be labor-intensive, but it'll be well worth the effort. Once in place, this path beckons visitors to explore the space beyond the garden gate. By using light-colored blocks, you'll ensure that the steps can be clearly seen day or night. A quick pass with a lawnmower will keep the steps safe for climbing.

Paving Materials

Driveways, paths and walkways are typically asphalt or concrete, which are poured all at once to form a monolithic slab. Contractors can dye or emboss concrete with decorative patterns for more visual appeal.

Pavers, on the other hand, are placed one at a time, often over a bed of compacted gravel and sand. Local stone yards or landscapers offer a variety of materials in many colors, sizes and price ranges. The most common choices are brick, stone and concrete, although increased interest in green building materials has led to a new option—pavers made from recycled plastic. All of these materials have pros and cons.

STYLE OPTIONS

In general, climate shouldn't be a concern when selecting pavers. Concrete, stone and kiln-fired brick all can handle weather's extremes. One consideration, however, is snow removal. Pavers that have become misaligned, or were set haphazardly in the first place, can snag the blade of a snow shovel or snow blower.

Aesthetically, pavers offer a wide range of decorative effects. Shapes range from precisely cut squares and rectangles to more organically shaped pieces that fit together like a jigsaw puzzle and give outdoor areas the feel of an informal English garden. Brick pavers are uniform in shape, if not in color, and often have a more formal, regimented look. Stone offers more variation in size, shape and coloring. Concrete is available in uniform shapes like bricks, or can be made to imitate the look of natural stone.

PRACTICAL MATTERS

Pavers take more time to install than a simple slab, and labor costs are consequently higher. But there are important advantages to installing this material: With all those joints, the surface is more flexible and therefore less likely to crack than concrete. If a paver does crack, or becomes stained or sinks out of alignment, it's easy to pop it out and replace or reset it.

In addition, the spaces between individual pavers give rain and snow melt a place to seep into the ground. This will earn you points if you're trying to get your home certified as green under the LEED (the U.S. Green Building Council's Leadership in Energy and Environmental Design) rating program. Runoff from parking lots, driveways and other impermeable surfaces can cause flooding while also washing pollutants into storm drains and local waterways. However, when water soaks back into the ground, it helps restore underground aquifers and reduces the load on municipal wastewater treatment plants. Some pavers—brick and composites—come in permeable versions to reduce runoff even more.

THE RIGHT BASE

Stone tile or brick can be set on a concrete base and the joints filled with mortar. The result is a more formal appearance, but it doesn't address the water-runoff issue, and the surface is susceptible to cracking like a poured surface. When placing pavers over a compacted base of gravel and sand, installers use a gas-driven compactor to vibrate the material into a dense, even field. Next is a thinner layer of sand or stone dust that's leveled with a long piece of lumber or metal called a screed. Pavers are set and leveled in this bed and joints are filled with the same sandy material, then swept or sprayed with a hose.

All of this prep work takes as much time and energy as setting the pavers themselves, maybe more. But without a good base, the surface is likely to develop sags, humps and other problems over time as the subsurface layer compacts. And a well-drained foundation for pavers lessens the chance of frost heaves.

No do-it-yourselfer will try to pour his own asphalt driveway—it takes heavy equipment and professional experience. But setting pavers requires simple tools and basic skills—well within the capacity of an industrious homeowner. It's a plus when you can offset the cost of materials with a little sweat equity. Instructions are easy to find (check just about any bookstore, library or home center) and the results will last for many years.

Calling In the Pros

If you are able and determined, you can lay a simple pathway yourself. Bigger projects require expert help. Here are some tips to help you decide if you should tackle the job or call in the pros.

- **PLACING A FEW STEPPING STONES** in the lawn is easy to do yourself. You can visit a stone yard and easily haul your finds back home in your car.
- **LARGE, FLAT ROCKS** are heavy and require muscle to move around. Enlist the help of some strong friends if you plan to place boulders or large slates in your yard yourself.
- **WALKWAYS LEADING TO THE FRONT DOOR** need to be mortared in place for safety. If you have experience working with cement, then you can attempt this type of path yourself; otherwise call a licensed stonemason.
- **INSTALLING STEEP STEPS,** cutting stone with a special saw and hauling heavy materials are jobs best left to professionals.
- **SOME STONE YARDS WILL DELIVER** materials to you, but you still need to move the stones into place. If you plan to handle this yourself, be sure you have a sturdy wheelbarrow on hand to help you do the job.

Inviting Outdoor Spaces
Porches, Patios, Decks

Porches, patios and decks can do much more than merely provide access or outdoor living space. Given the right choice of materials, these surfaces can help control flooding, replenish underground water supplies and even reduce the number of old tires and plastic bottles clogging local landfills. All that, and they keep your shoes from getting muddy. The images on the pages that follow show how a collection of creative homeowners and designers created outdoor living spaces that increased the value and curb appeal of their homes without breaking the bank.

above Designer Amanda Sandberg replaced the small backyard of this California cottage with a swimming pool surrounded by a slate patio and added a whirlpool and a shade cabana over a pair of chaises, too. She also enclosed the porch that leads out to the pool area, but linked it to the outdoor areas by using the same slate paving stones inside and out. left To brighten the covered porch of her Hamptons weekend house, designer Libby Langdon whitewashed the decking boards and created a cozy seating area with wicker furnishings topped with cushions covered in a lively floral and striped indoor/outdoor fabrics. "I love creating spaces where guests can escape for private, quiet time," says Libby. Potted geraniums add shots of vibrant color.

Decking Materials

SHOPPING FOR DECKING

When planning a new deck, it's crucial that you select materials that will stand the test of time. For many, the hardest part of building a deck is choosing which material to use. Today, homeowners have many more choices than even a few years ago. However, once you understand what's out there, the selection process isn't that difficult. To make it less bewildering, here's a summary of the essence of what's available:

WOOD

Wood still accounts for nearly 80 percent of all the decks built today, and for good reason. Treated wood is readily available in every lumberyard and home center, and, at least initially, costs less than the other decking materials. (Regardless of what's on top, most deck frames are built from treated southern pine because of its winning combination of strength, rot resistance and low cost.)

To protect decking from termites and decay, wood was once impregnated with chromated copper arsenate (CCA). This was found to be carcinogenic and, when the EPA banned it in 2003, manufacturers switched to arsenic-free preservative treatments, such as copper azole (CA) and alkaline copper quarternary (ACQ). These new chemicals don't affect the performance or appearance of wood (freshly treated boards still have a greenish tinge) and are safer for people.

It's worth pointing out that preservatives don't prevent all possible problems. Rain and sunlight conspire to create a host of damage, such as swelling, shrinking, warping and splitting. To prevent premature aging and keep your deck looking its best, you'll need to clean and protect the wood with a clear water-repellent sealer or semitransparent deck stain about once a year.

Because it's milled from fast-growing trees, standard-grade pressure-treated pine can appear knotty, and may move or split as it dries out. For a richer look, you can spend more on a higher grade or step up to redwood or cedar. Forest Stewardship Council–certified lumber (lumber legally harvested from environmentally responsible forests) is available; however, shipping costs make this material expensive for East Coast residents. Cedar and redwood also require regular cleaning and sealing, and will eventually fade to a silvery gray.

Ipe, an imported hardwood that's naturally resistant to rot and insect damage, is a fairly new decking option. Like cedar and redwood, the freshly sawn reddish brown boards will fade, but unlike its domestic competition, ipe does not require annual sealing.

COMPOSITES

In the 1990s, the Trex company combined wood fiber and plastic for a new decking material. This innovative combination offers the longevity of plastic in a product that looks and works like wood. Today, wood/plastic composites dominate the low-maintenance decking market; at last count there were more than 60 brands, all offering their own assortment of colors and textures.

Based on their chemical makeup, composites fall into two sub-categories: polyethylene composites and polypropylene composites. Polyethylene composites (such as ChoiceDek, TimberTech and Trex) dominate the market. These boards feel solid underfoot, but the softer plastic means joists must be spaced closer than they are with wood. This makes it difficult to replace wood with composite on

top left Western red cedar decking is beautiful, lightweight and easy to work with; plus, it's naturally resistant to insects and harsh weather. *wrcla.org.*

above Composite decking is as easy to work with as wood, but the flexibility of some brands, like Trex, lets builders create more curves. *trex.com.*

above Plastic and vinyl decking, such as Eon, avoid the maintenance issues of wood and is fully recyclable. *eonoutdoor.com.*

like siding, most of the other wood-free products—Bear Board, Dek Lock—resemble composites. A few, like Eon and Procell, look like real wood.

The installation of plastic planks varies widely. Vinyl isn't difficult to cut, but installation requires special clips, caps and detail pieces, while composites can be cut and installed much like wood, although some offer special fasteners.

ALUMINUM

This heavy-gauge metal decking may be the most expensive option, but for good reason. Aluminum offers advantages that you can't find in the other choices. It's maintenance-free, lightweight and ideal for rooftop decks. The interlocking panels create a gutter system that channels water away, and it can serve as a roof for usable space below.

Installing aluminum decking imposes some design limitations. It also requires different tools and nonferrous metal–cutting blades. Compared to wood, cutting metal is noisy and slow. The best way to minimize the noise (and expense) of off-cuts is to design your deck's frame to fit full-length panels.

an old deck. On the plus side, builders can take advantage of the boards' flexibility and create curves that would be impossible with wood.

Polypropylene composites (such as CrossTimbers and CorrectDeck) are made with a stiffer plastic, so boards can span longer distances. These manufacturers can offer hollow boards that weigh less. The disadvantage of hollow boards is that concealing exposed ends and making sure that ripped edges are properly reinforced requires extra effort.

The biggest problem with composites is their price. The material cost for a composite deck runs from two to five times more than for pressure-treated wood. However, the annual maintenance costs for wood—cleaning, staining, sealing—can offset the higher initial price of a composite in less than five years, especially if you plan on hiring a pro to build your deck. Builders often prefer working with composites because the lack of defects makes for a faster, cleaner job. The clips, brackets and precut parts that come with composite rail systems make it possible to install an 8-foot railing section in minutes. By saving time, composite decks cost less to build. So, synthetic decks may still cost 25 to 50 percent more, but the money goes underfoot rather than in a builder's pocket. And the added value of a maintenance-free deck may help when it's time to sell.

VINYL AND OTHER PLASTICS

Wood-free plastic planks eliminate the inherent disadvantages of wood, such as mold and moisture-related problems. Plastic decking requires even less maintenance than composites; most manufacturers recommend little more than an occasional rinsing with a garden hose. While some vinyl decking products look more

deck boards, side by side

	COST PER SQ. FT.	ADVANTAGES	DISADVANTAGES	AVERAGE LIFESPAN
PRESSURE-TREATED WOOD	■ $2–$4	■ Economical ■ Readily available ■ Easy to work with ■ Can be stained	■ Annual maintenance recommended ■ Boards may split or warp	■ 15 years
CEDAR, REDWOOD	■ $3–$6	■ Naturally insect- and rot-resistant ■ Easy to work with ■ Can be stained	■ Annual maintenance recommended ■ Sapwood not as resistant as heartwood	■ 15–20 years
IPE	■ $5	■ Little to no maintenance ■ Naturally insect- and rot-resistant	■ Predrilling required	■ 40 years
COMPO-SITES	■ $4–$6	■ Little maintenance ■ Some made from recycled plastics ■ Boards can be bent around curves	■ Some require closer joist spacing ■ Some look "plasticky" ■ Heavier than wood	■ 10–25 years (warranties vary)
VINYL AND OTHER 100% PLASTICS	■ $5–$7	■ Little maintenance ■ Lightweight products easier to handle	■ Some products do not resemble wood ■ Some sound "hollow" when walked on	■ 20 years (warranties vary)
ALUMINUM	■ $7	■ No maintenance ■ Creates roof and deck ■ Fireproof	■ Expensive ■ Difficult to design custom-shaped decks	■ Lifetime (warranties vary)

left This 1960s Palm Beach house, with its butterfly roof, already had a nice floor plan and inviting outdoor pool area. As an upgrade, its owner, Rudy Calvero, installed sliding glass doors to replace French doors, substantially opening the living room onto the patio. A new roof added over part of the patio shields it from the desert sun and creates the ambience of an outdoor room. To complete the patio with a retro look, Rudy added white plastic chairs and a sleek table from Ikea. He also surrounded the pool with vintage 1950s lounge chairs in blue, yellow and white.

above The deck of Designer Jeff Lewis's home in Los Feliz, California, is built around a tree, which contributes to the tree-house feeling Jeff loves. He has 180-degree views of the canyons, nearby Los Angeles and, on a clear day, the ocean. Sleek woven outdoor furniture fitted with plump cushions provides comfortable seating for guests when Jeff entertains.

right Architect Joseph Eisner added two new slatted mahogany cabana structures linked by a pergola and 4x4-inch stone pavers to upgrade the poolside area of a house in the Hamptons. One is a shower/changing room, the other is for storage. bottom right The home's new deck, with built-in seating and grill, is also constructed of mahogany. The stainless steel cable railing suggests a nautical theme. Eisner designed the dining table.

above This prefabricated 1960s modern home is one of 450 houses in the Hollin Hills neighborhood of Alexandria, Virginia, designed by architect Charles Goodman. Owner Eric Johnson and his wife rebuilt the decks and planted native grasses.

Budget-Wise Concrete Tips

While the economy was ailing, many homeowners opted to cut back on remodeling expenses and forgo home improvement projects. But installing a decorative concrete patio, sidewalk or entryway can be done fairly simply without putting a major dent in your pocketbook. You can spend a premium for elaborate stamped, stenciled or multicolored concrete, but you can also achieve equally impressive results with these three budget-friendly decorative treatments, recommended by the Concrete Network. These approaches will save you money and also give you a durable, low-maintenance surface that will last for decades.

- **EXPOSED AGGREGATE** You can achieve wonderful effects with an exposed aggregate finish at a reasonable price because few additional materials are required. To get the look, a contractor simply places the concrete and then removes the top layer of cement paste by scrubbing or pressure-washing to reveal an embedded aggregate. Many types and sizes of decorative aggregate are available to achieve any number of color and textural variations. Ideal for most exterior flatwork, an exposed-aggregate finish is durable and skid-resistant, too.
- **ROCK SALT FINISH** A traditional and easy way to add subtle texture and skid resistance to plain or colored concrete is with a rock salt finish. The salt leaves a speckled pattern of shallow indentations on the concrete surface, like the slightly pitted appearance of weathered rock. Salt finishes are naturally appealing alone, but can also be used in combination with colored concrete and other decorative treatments. This finish requires few additional tools and materials to produce, keeping the cost affordable.
- **BROOMING AND BORDERS** On a tight budget, you can achieve interesting decorative results by mixing stamped or stenciled concrete borders with fields of less-expensive plain or broom-finished concrete.

Tips on Painting or Staining Concrete

If you want to paint or stain an existing concrete surface, follow these recommendations from the Concrete Network:

- **PAINTING CONCRETE** is normally only considered when it is required to cover an existing slab. For instance, after a crack has been repaired and then a concrete colorant can be used to cover the blemish.
- **FOR EXTERIOR AREAS** that receive heavy foot traffic, the paint often wears away and the area will need repainting.
- **FRESH CONCRETE SHOULD NEVER BE PAINTED.** Allow the concrete to cure for at least 28 days—follow the paint manufacturer's recommendations.
- **DO NOT APPLY CURING COMPOUNDS** to concrete that will be painted. It will cause problems allowing the paint to bond to the concrete.
- **USE CONCRETE PAINT,** sometimes referred to as cement paint. This type of paint breathes, allowing any moisture that comes up through the concrete to vaporize and not become trapped beneath the surface causing the paint to blister.
- **BEFORE CONCRETE CAN BE PAINTED,** dirt, oil and efflorescence must be removed from it.
- **ON NEW CONCRETE,** stain manufacturers recommend letting the concrete cure for at least 30 days before applying a stain, and avoiding the use of curing compounds.
- **ON EXISTING CONCRETE,** keep in mind that stains are intended to enhance rather than disguise the surface. They will not mask cracks, blemishes, discoloration or other flaws. An existing concrete slab with major cracks or spalling is usually not a good candidate for staining because any patchwork is likely to show right through the stain. A solution to this problem is to cover the concrete with a thin cement-based overlay to create a fresh new canvas to work on.
- **THE COST OF STAINING VARIES CONSIDERABLY** depending on the complexity of the stain application, surface prep requirements, the size of the job, the type of sealer used and your local market. In general, a basic one-coat application of stain with sealer and minimal surface prep will run about $2 to $4 per square foot. More elaborate stain projects incorporating faux finishing, multiple colors, and designs or borders can run much higher (about $15 per square foot or more).
- **GENERALLY, THERE ARE TWO CATEGORIES OF CONCRETE STAINS**—reactive and nonreactive. Reactive stains are chemical stains—water-based acidic solutions containing metallic salts that react with the concrete's lime content. Once the chemical reaction takes place, the stain forms a permanent bond with the concrete and won't chip off or peel away. Nonreactive stains are water-based acrylic stains that don't rely on a chemical reaction to impart color. Instead, they are formulated to penetrate the concrete surface and deposit their pigment particles in the open pores. Nonreactive stains have become popular over the past few years because they come in a much broader palette of colors than acid stains and are easier to apply. The downside: They don't produce the same variegated, translucent color tones characteristic of acid stains. Instead, their color effects are more opaque and uniform.

For more information on concrete stains and cleaning tips, visit *concretenetwork.com*.

BEFORE

above The pitched roofline hemmed in the second floor. Plantings near the house seemed haphazardly arranged. **left** A bump-out in the roof made room for second-level bedrooms and dramatically increased interior square footage. Outside, a new deck was added to extend the living area outdoors, and new planters were added in front of new windows to enrich the view. **opposite top** When interior designer Pamela Hill and architect Lois Mackenzie found a 1940s two-bedroom "beach shack," some of the local builders they spoke to recommended tearing it down: It needed too much work. But the two women were not about to see their diamond-in-the-rough dream house carted off to the dump. With an owner-held mortgage in hand, they found a simpatico contractor and went to work. Luckily, the roof was in good shape, but they needed to install new windows, wiring, plumbing, floors and a deck. Then they reclad the exterior with natural cedar shingles. To take advantage of dramatic views of the ocean, they added new decks of Western red cedar off the front and side of the house. The simple woven chairs are from Ikea. **opposite bottom left** The view from the new back deck of this home takes in the densely wooded setting. The new master suite could pass for a grownup tree house. **opposite right center** A new addition turned the square house into an L-shape, taking advantage of the deep lot. Its roof, a cool eco feature, sheds rain into a gutter system that waters the garden. **opposite right bottom** Before its renovation, the house was boxy and boring.

Exterior Upgrades

Giving the facade of your home a facelift can work wonders for its curb appeal. Sometimes all that's needed is a fresh coat of paint. In other cases, heavier-duty rehabs are in order—an addition, new siding, a bump-out or substantial landscape improvements. The projects featured on the pages that follow offer inspired approaches to improving the exteriors of old houses cost-effectively—and often with sensitivity to the environment.

LINKING BUMP-OUTS AND ENRICHING GARDENS

A 1980s house (pictured above) in the Hamptons recently renovated by architect Joseph Eisner was sorely in need of a facelift. "I wanted to create an indoor/outdoor garden sensibility," says the architect. The renovation included a major makeover of the outdoor areas and the exterior, too. The second floor bump-outs and chimney were clad in stucco. A mahogany deck with a built-in grill and seating seems to extend the living room into the trees. The landscape got some tailoring with planters made of rusticated, engineered, stone that form the crisp border from house and deck to pool. And beside the pool, two mahogany slat cabanas (not shown), linked by a pergola, provide storage and space for showers and changing, and gracefully merge indoor and outdoor living.

BEFORE

STRETCHING A HOUSE UP AND DOWN

After their daughters were born, Katie and Joe Morford's 1908 San Francisco home (right) felt like it started to shrink. It had been a compact one-story house with a basement and an unfinished attic space. A small, inefficient kitchen and dining area were added to the back in the '80s; a master bedroom and bath had been built over the kitchen, but the existing attic was left unfinished. And like many San Francisco homes, there was no garage or off-street parking. The plan architect Andrew Mann devised would require 18 months, from initial planning through completion. The front yard's elevation made it possible to tunnel directly into the basement from the street to create a tuck-under garage. The first floor's basic configuration was good, too, with the exception of the layout of the kitchen. Creating the second-story addition required some major work. The bedroom above the kitchen stayed in place, becoming a family room—"It's where we watch TV and play games together," Katie says—and the existing master bath was renovated for the girls' use. But Mann had the front two-thirds of the roof torn off to make use of the unfinished attic as usable second-floor space. The new addition now houses two bedrooms for the three girls, a master suite and bath in front, and a convenient laundry room, which includes a sunny window. To bring more light into the upstairs interior, Mann turned the hallway ceiling into a skylight. Transoms above the doorways to bedrooms and baths add a period touch that also allows light to filter between spaces.

The home's exterior underwent a significant transformation, but because of Mann's attention to blending old and new, it looks as if the original has remained untouched. The nicest compliment, Mann recalls, came from a cousin who drove by with him to check out the project. Says Mann, "She looked up at the house and asked, 'What did you do?'"

above Excavating the yard and converting the basement into a garage gave the owners of this home valuable off-street parking. The wood siding on the second-floor addition was matched to the existing exterior.
left The old exterior was quaint and charming, although the tiny front yard didn't provide the homeowners with usable space.

left Architect Charles Moore calls the additions to this 1940s Washington, DC, area house as "the village" because they make it look like a series of small buildings. The new, Arts and Crafts–inspired facade is clad in fiber-cement siding and cedar shingles.

above With its reconfigured sides, new cedar shingles and white trim, an old A-frame now has a traditional look that suits its environs in East Hampton, New York. Owner Elaine Dia and her husband, Scott, expanded the living room and added a porch deck that runs along the full width of the house, which also got a new entrance. The side porch connects the guest bath to the pool area.

top right The canopy over the office entrance of an urban structure renovated with environmentally friendly approaches by architect Rick Renner is planted with golden thread cypress. A solar panel adjoins the rooftop garden, or green roof, which is accessed from a new bump-up above the study. The exterior brick is original. **right** A low-maintenance and stylish green roof garden covers a third of the roof and is planted with sedum in gravel-filled trays. The plants winter over nicely, and have tripled in size since they were first planted. The green roof also insulates the building and helps to manage rainwater runoff. "I'm a gardener," says Rick's wife, Janet. "Since we don't have a yard, I have the rooftop and the canopies over the doors." The roof also holds a solar panel to offset utility costs.

creating curb appeal and inviting outdoor spaces 139

Case Studies
Case Study 1: Inviting Patio Makeover

Built in 1937, this stucco-sided house in West Toluca Lake, California, was backed by a small, sparse concrete patio. After owning the house for a few years, Richard G. Murphy decided that his outdoor space was wasted. Though he'd arranged chairs around an umbrella-topped table, it had little alfresco appeal and was rarely used.

Richard replaced the cracked surface with a redwood deck on concrete footings, putting the patio on the same level as the house. To make the space feel more roomlike, he enclosed it with redwood railings, low hedges and tall pillars supporting a pergola. Fast-growing trumpet vines will climb the pillars and weave their way across the top, making a leafy ceiling. Bothered by the windowless house wall facing his new deck, Richard hung up a 4x5-foot mirror. Now anyone sitting there can view the rest of the landscaped quarter-acre property without twisting. And the mirror reflects sunlight as well as the pleasing view.

Things to Think About

- **TRANSITIONS** A single step connects the patio to a path leading to the driveway and garage on the right, gardens on the left. Both the step and path are brick laid in a basket-weave pattern.
- **FINISHES** Knowing it would soon be covered, Richard simply stained the pergola white. "But the pillars and railings were painted in high-gloss enamel. I wanted to be able to keep up that shiny wet look I like," he says.
- **FURNISHINGS** A wooden bench, lounges, chairs and tables, even a rug, add to the feeling that this is an outdoor room. "I can actually accommodate more guests here than in my living room," says Richard.

above With its cracked concrete slab and lack of shade, the old patio was stark and uninviting. **left** A raised redwood deck and soon-to-be-vine-covered pergola helped turn the space into a welcoming oasis.

Case Study 2: Low-Cost Roof Deck Redo

The 15 residents of this Atlanta loft-style building never imagined chic dinner parties could be thrown just a few flights up from their apartments, where 360-degree views of the city skyline and twinkling lights can be enjoyed from the rooftop. The outside space—with its broken deck boards and shaky railing—was downright dangerous. But resident Brian Patrick Flynn, an interior designer on HGTV's *Decorating Cents* and TBS's *Movie & a Makeover,* saw possibilities. "I'm home most of the time," says Flynn. "I was frustrated that we never used it."

In just five days, Flynn hauled out the old and brought in the new. With a nod to his favorite boutique hotel designers—Kelly Wearstler and Jonathan Adler—he created an eclectic 750-square-foot space with bold, bright colors and funky revamped flea-market furniture that would suit the tastes of the young neighbors that live in the 12-unit former warehouse. First, the deck boards were replaced and painted in a Greek key pattern to define the dining area. To satisfy building codes that prohibited building a permanent pergola, Flynn devised a four-poster table with an overhead arbor to hold an electrified chandelier that casts a soft glow over the table. Acrylic "grass," resistant to pests and mold, was installed under a seating area flanked by planter boxes filled with colorful tropical and succulent plants, which were chosen for their ability to withstand sun, wind and heat. The result is an upscale outdoor dining area that rivals the poshest places in town.

What Was Done

- **REMOVED** cracked decking, broken planters and worn-out furniture.
- **REPLACED** deck boards and adorned them with marine-grade paint in a Greek key pattern.
- **ADDED** a drainage system so rainwater runs into rain barrels for watering plants.
- **BUILT** planters and filled them with soil, colorful succulents and tropical plants.
- **CONSTRUCTED** a four-poster table/arbor, and painted and reupholstered furniture with marine vinyl to shed water.
- **INSTALLED** acrylic grass and painted the fiberglass containers red to match color scheme.

BEFORE

left With seating for 10, the newly designed dining area is the perfect spot for hosting large parties and taking in the spectacular views of downtown Atlanta. above The sun-baked decking and furniture was less than welcoming for residents and guests of the building. below The garden cocktail area offers comfortable seating with a faux-grass carpet underfoot and colorful plants that can endure the hot Georgia summers.

Case Study 3: Garden Makeover

BEFORE

When homeowners Bryan and Brooke Crane added on to their 1926 Los Angeles cottage to create a master bedroom suite, the view from the new room looked out on their boring driveway. "We wanted to look at trees and plants instead," said Brooke. For a solution, the couple turned to Ann Meshekoff, owner of Ground Effects Design Group, in Van Nuys, California, and her design team to come up with a plan. With a limited budget, Meshekoff suggested preserving most of the existing landscape—but adding to it.

Bryan, who works in real-estate finance, wanted architectural-looking plants with spiky leaves and interesting shapes. Brooke, a stay-at-home mom, wanted a softer look reminiscent of an English country garden that would go with the style of their home.

above Construction of a 250-square-foot addition to the house expanded the master bedroom but left a barren yard with no view. below A melange of plants soften the new flagstone pathway, inviting visitors to explore.

Meshekoff poured over books and garden magazines with the couple until they arrived at a compromise. Above all, the yard had to be safe for their new baby and the dog.

At approximately 8,000 square feet, the level property already had a garden scheme with pathways and patios, but the look just didn't flow cohesively from the front yard to the back. So the plan was to punch it up and link both parts of the yard. The broken brick patio and wobbly walkways were removed. Trees planted too close together were cut down, and the driveway—leading to a garage that was turned into a utility/studio space—was shortened. Drainage on the site was improved by grading the soil and installing a sump pump.

Once the groundwork was done, Meshekoff began crafting her gardenscape by carving out curving walkways, adding a new patio and installing large, irregularly shaped flagstones to define an outdoor living room. The paths now lead from the back door of the house to the studio, an office outbuilding, a dining area under a pittosporum tree strung with lights and a hot tub under an existing pergola. Purple-leafed plum trees were planted to match

above A large pittosporum tree shades the backyard and pergola that houses a Jacuzzi hot tub. below The garage was repurposed as a utility/studio space, so the driveway was shortened. Undulating pathways of natural stone now lead from a cocktail patio to a dining space under the trees and over to the hot tub for a relaxing soak. right A cozy outdoor living room furnished with plush seating was created on the new stone patio in front of the studio. Colorful plants in flower beds and flower-filled containers invite all to enjoy the garden.

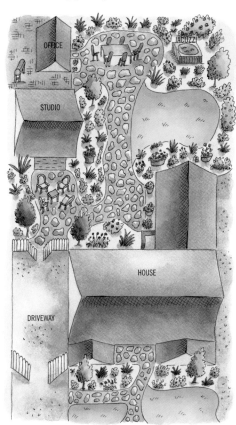

those in the front yard, along with citrus trees, birches and a cherry tree. Several rose bushes, which had been saved from the original garden, were surrounded by hydrangeas, camellias, phormiums (for the spiky leaves Bryan loves) and acanthus plants.

Next came a layer of perennials, including artemisia, scented geraniums, gardenias, Japanese anemones and daylilies, chosen for their color and fragrance—and because they'd be nontoxic to the dog and baby. Finally, ground covers were planted to fill in the spaces. Herbs, including rosemary, lavender, basil, chives and thyme, were interspersed among the beds to add a loose, country garden look. "We did a lot of repetition," said Meshekoff. "So the front yard would 'talk' to the rear."

With new outdoor lighting, the yard is now used both day and night for entertaining. Cocktails are served on the patio with guests seated in plush chairs; dinner parties are hosted on another patio under the trees. After taking care to match their new bedroom to the English style of the home, the Cranes' new garden enhances the Old World feeling.

Sources

ARCHITECTS AND DESIGNERS

Andrew Mann Architecture
Andrewmannarchitecture.com

The Breakfast Room, Ltd.
Thebreakfastroom.com

Brian Patrick Flynn
Brianpatrickflynn.com

Christine Donner Kitchen Design
Donnerkitchens.com

Company kd
Companykd.com

Donna DuFresne Design
Donnadufresnedesign.com

Eileen Kathryn Boyd Interiors
Ekbinteriors.com

Eisner Design
Eisnerdesign.com

Erica Broberg Smith, Architect
Ericabrobergarchitect.com

Ground Effects Design Group
Groundeffectsdesigngroup.com

Home ReBuilders
www.homerebuilders.com

Jeff Lewis Design
Jefflewisdesign.com

Jessica Helgerson Interior Design
Jhinteriordesign.com

Joanne Hans
Aperfectplacement.com

Kate Singer Home
Katesingerhome.com

Libby Langdon
Libbylangdon.com

Lois Mackenzie
Ottobaat.com

Michael Roberson Interior Design
Michaelroberson.com

Moore Architects
Moorearch.com

Nantucket Architecture Group
Nantucketarchitecture.com

Omniarte Design
Omniartedesign.com

Pamela Hill
Ottobaat.com

Renner Architects
Rennerarchitects.com

Scott Martin
Blueplumdesign.com

T. Keller Donovan Inc.
212-760-0537

Tineke Triggs
Artisticdesignsforliving.com

Todd Pritchett Design Studio
Toddpritchettdesignstudio.com

Yianni Doulis Architecture Studio
Ydarchitecture.com

ASSOCIATIONS AND ORGANIZATIONS

Catalogchoice.org

Concrete Network
Concretenetwork.com

Consumersearch.com

U.S. Consumer Product Safety Commission
Cpsc.gov

Eartheasy.com

Efficient Windows Collaborative
Efficientwindows.org

Energystar.gov

Epa.gov

Forest Stewardship Council
Fsc.org

Greenseal.org

National Kitchen & Bath Association
Nkba.org

Western Red Cedar Lumber Association
Wrcla.org

World Floor Covering Association
Wfca.org

MANUFACTURERS

Ann Sacks
annsacks.com

Avonite
Avonitesurfaces.com

Behr
Behr.com

Benjamin Moore
Benjaminmoore.com

Bona
Bona.com

Brunschwig & Fils
Brunschwig.com

Caesar Stone
Caesarstone.com

CalicoCorners
Calicocorners.com

ChoiceDek
Choicedek.com

Christopher Peacock Home
Peacockcabinetry.com

Corian
DuPont.com

CorrectDeck
Correctdeck.com

CrossTimbers
Gaf.com

Dal-Tile
Daltile.com

Duralee
Duralee.com

Eon
Eonoutdoor.com

General Electric
Ge.com

Glidden
Glidden.com

Heath Ceramics
Heathceramics.com

Honeywell
Honeywell.com

Kolbe & Kolbe
Kolbe-kolbe.com

Lutron
Lutron.com

Moen
Moen.com

Monster Cable
Monstercable.com

Panasonic
Panasonic.com

Rohl
Rohlhome.com

Sherwin-Williams
Sherwin-williams.com

Sunbrella
Sunbrella.com

Swanstone
Theswancorp.com

Thermador
Thermador.com

TimberTech
Timbertech.com

Trex
Trex.com

TruStile
TruStile.com

Viking
Vikingrange.com

Wolf
Wolfappliance.com

RETAILERS

Ballard Designs
Ballarddesigns.com

Bed Bath & Beyond
Bedbathandbeyond.com

The Container Store
Containerstore.com

Country Curtains
Countrycurtains.com

The Home Depot
homedepot.com

HomeGoods
homegoods.com

Ikea
Ikea.com

Modern Nursery
Modernnursery.com

Pottery Barn
Potterybarn.com

Restoration Hardware
Restorationhardware.com

T.J. Maxx
Tjmaxx.com

West Elm
Westelm.com

Acknowledgements

The talent and energy of several people went into the making of this book and all deserve our acknowledgment and thanks. Much of the information contained in these pages was gleaned through reporting done by several staff editors and regular contributors to the *Woman's Day* Special Interest Publications, including Bernadette Baczynski, Leslie Clagett, Megan Fulweiler, Scott Gibson, Chris Hughes, Jill Kirchner Simpson, John Loecke, Ginevra Pylant, Kelly Tagore, Ayn-Monique Tetreault-Rooney Klahre, Karen Walden, Peter Walsh, William Weathersby, Jr., and Carolyn Weber. A number of stylists have also contributed to much of the visual content in these pages, including Sarah Alba, Andrea Caughey, Anne Gridley, Sunday Hendrickson, Audrey Lee, Ingrid Leess, Marie Moss, Donna Pizzi, Gisela Rose, Donna Talley and Erinn Valencich. We are grateful to all. Special thanks also goes to Matthew Levinson for his photo direction and production assistance. Finally, our gratitude goes to Dorothée Walliser for shepherding the book through its development and publication.